OCCASIONAL PAPER 231

Chile
Institutions and Policies Underpinning Stability and Growth

Eliot Kalter, Steven Phillips, Marco A. Espinosa-Vega,
Rodolfo Luzio, Mauricio Villafuerte, and Manmohan Singh

INTERNATIONAL MONETARY FUND
Washington DC
2004

OCCASIONAL PAPER 231

Chile
Institutions and Policies Underpinning Stability and Growth

Eliot Kalter, Steven Phillips, Marco A. Espinosa-Vega, Rodolfo Luzio, Mauricio Villafuerte, and Manmohan Singh

INTERNATIONAL MONETARY FUND
Washington DC
2004

© 2004 International Monetary Fund

Production: IMF Multimedia Services Division

Figures: Theodore F. Peters, Jr.
Typesetting: Alicia Etchebarne-Bourdin

Cataloging-in-Publication Data

Chile: institutions and policies underpinning stability and growth/Eliot
Kalter . . . [et al]—Washington, D.C.: International Monetary Fund, 2004.

p. cm.—(Occasional paper, 231, 0251-6365; 231)

Includes bibliographical references.

ISBN 1589063252

1. Chile—Economic policy. 2. Capital market—Chile. 3. Banks and
banking—Chile. I. Kalter, Eliot. II. Occasional paper (International Monetary Fund); 231.

HC 192.5.C45 2004

Price: US$25.00
(US$22.00 to full-time faculty members and
students at universities and colleges)

Please send orders to:
International Monetary Fund, Publication Services
700 19th Street, N.W., Washington, D.C. 20431, U.S.A.
Tel.: (202) 623-7430   Telefax: (202) 623-7201
E-mail: publications@imf.org
Internet: http://www.imf.org

recycled paper

Contents

Figures

The following symbols have been used throughout this paper:

. . .   to indicate that data are not available;

—   to indicate that the figure is zero or less than half the final digit shown, or that the item does not exist;

–   between years or months (e.g., 2003–04 or January–June) to indicate the years or months covered, including the beginning and ending years or months;

/   between years (e.g., 2003/04) to indicate a fiscal (financial) year.

"n.a." means not applicable.

"Billion" means a thousand million.

Minor discrepancies between constituent figures and totals are due to rounding.

The term "country," as used in this paper, does not in all cases refer to a territorial entity that is a state as understood by international law and practice; the term also covers some territorial entities that are not states, but for which statistical data are maintained and provided internationally on a separate and independent basis.

Preface

Most of the material presented in this occasional paper was originally prepared as a selected issues paper for discussion at the IMF Executive Board. These selected issues reviewed the institutions and policies adopted by Chile in the past two decades that have enabled it to reduce its vulnerabilities while benefiting from the ongoing process of globalization.

The idea of publishing these issues as an occasional paper arose from the Executive Board's suggestion that this collection could provide a unified source of lessons for countries that, like Chile, are committed to undertake sustainable improvements to their economic policies and institutions. Since the publication is intended as a reference, it also includes some forward-looking suggestions.

The authors are grateful to the Chilean authorities for extensive and open discussions as well as for their assistance in providing data and other source material, and to a number of commentators for their patient feedback: Governor Vittorio Corbo, Finance Minister Nicolas Eyzaguirre, Economy Minister Jorge Rodríguez, Executive Director Guillermo LeFort, Antonio Ahumada, Jaime Crispi, Luis Eduardo Escobar, Helmut Franken, Rodrigo Fuentes, Leonardo Hernandez, Luis Oscar Herrera, Esteban Jadresic, Igal Magendzo, Mario Marcel, Jorge Perez, Bernardita Piedrabuena, Luis Salomo, Claudio Sapelli, Klaus Schmidt-Hebbel, Rodrigo Valdes, and seminar participants at the Central Bank of Chile. Finally, the authors are grateful to Andrew Swiston, without whose invaluable support this occasional paper could not have been prepared; Carmen Sanabia and Gloria Bustillo for their assistance in the preparation of the manuscript; and Esha Ray of the External Relations Department for coordinating production of the publication.

The opinions expressed in this paper are solely those of the authors and do not necessarily reflect the views of the IMF, its Executive Directors, or the Chilean authorities.

I   Overview

Eliot Kalter

Throughout much of the twentieth century, Chile's economic performance was marked by low economic growth and high inflation. In sharp contrast, in the last twenty years Chile has enjoyed a strong and stable economy while the economies of many of its Latin American neighbors have stagnated and suffered repeated financial crises.

The remarkable turnaround of the Chilean economy reflects the authorities' sustained implementation of a broad range of policies, enabling the country to take advantage of an increasingly global environment that has presented dangers to other, less well-prepared countries. As recently noted by Carlos Massad,[1] the widespread disenchantment of the Chilean people with the policies and outcomes of much of the twentieth century set the stage for a major shift in policies. The Chilean authorities took advantage of this historic moment by taking difficult decisions to form a solid foundation for the future.

This occasional paper presents the primary institutions and economic policies that have led to Chile's sucessful record of stability and growth. The paper highlights the institutional factors that have enabled the Chilean authorities to sustain good policies over a long and particularly difficult period for many of its neighbors. It is apparent that the core of this policy stance is the combination of fiscal discipline and an open trade policy regime, coupled with carefully sequenced financial liberalization within a strengthened regulatory framework. These policies have been sustained—despite external and domestic forces to the contrary—because of carefully designed institutional arrangements that encourage policies oriented toward long-term success, shielding policymakers from the temptation to look for narrow or short-term gains at the potential cost of long-term stability.

Chile's long-term policy framework has protected its economy from the negative impact of "stop-go" capital flows that has accompanied financial globalization for many emerging market countries.[2] As a result, Chile has been able to take advantage of the increased growth prospects, stemming from its open external trade and capital markets without giving back these gains during financial crises.

Economic Performance

As Figure 1.1 illustrates, economic performance in Chile in the last two decades has been impressive in relation to other countries in the region.

- *Trend economic growth was faster in Chile (top left panel).* From 1984 to 1997 economic activity in Chile grew at an annual rate exceeding 7 percent, and was much faster in Chile than in other countries on average. Back in 1980, per capita income (adjusted on the basis of purchasing power parity) in Chile had been significantly below that of Argentina, essentially the same as Mexico's and not much above Brazil's. Two decades later, Chilean income was far ahead of the others' (twice that of Brazil, and over one and a half times those of Argentina and Mexico).

- *Economic growth was also smoother in Chile (top right panel).* Only Chile avoided a major episode of output contraction in the last 20 years. Chile's last crisis episode, in 1982, was however the worst of the group—only Argentina's decline in 2002 comes close. As discussed in Section II, this 1982 crisis proved a watershed for Chile, playing a critical role in reorienting economic policies and institutions.

- *Inflation was lower—and also less volatile—in Chile (middle panels).* From 20 percent in 1990, annual inflation declined steadily, down to 6 percent in 1997, and reaching the low single digits a few years ago.

---

[1]Massad (2003).

[2]Calvo and Reinhart (2000).

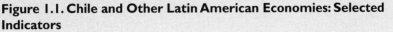

Figure 1.1. Chile and Other Latin American Economies: Selected Indicators

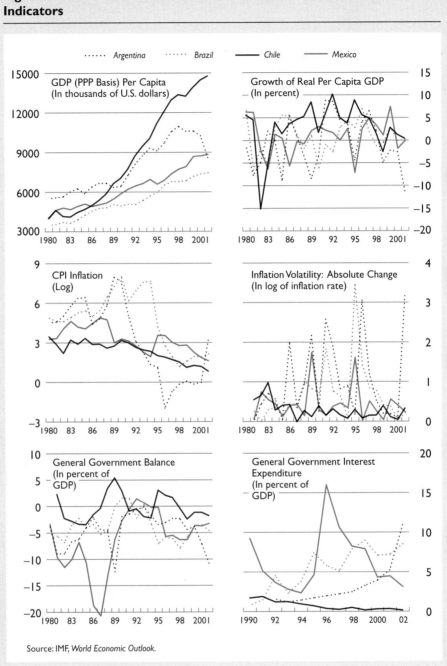

Source: IMF, *World Economic Outlook.*

Policies Underpinning Success

Several economic and financial policies and institutional arrangements seem especially key to Chile's success:

- *Fiscal discipline has been strong in Chile.* Looking over the last two decades, only in Chile were years of fiscal deficits roughly offset by years of surpluses; most Latin American countries displayed a bias toward deficits. As also shown in Figure 1.1, the reward has been a vastly lower debt-servicing burden for Chile, as fiscal discipline resulted not only in lower government debt but also in lower real interest rates.

• *The financial regulatory framework was strengthened and a deepening of domestic capital markets was encouraged.* Financial liberalization was a mainstay of policy reform in Latin America in the 1990s, mainly focusing on deregulation and privatization. However, supporting regulatory frameworks remained inadequate. Chile took strong actions to try to strike the right balance of market discipline and sound banking supervision.

• *Trade integration, in conjunction with a broad financial opening, was significant.*

—Chile's export sector, one of the most open and diversified in Latin America, has proven an important buffer against current account shocks. In general, Latin America's trade sector is relatively small, and exports are often concentrated in a few commodities. This has increased the region's vulnerabilities to current account shocks due to the high ratio of foreign debt to exports and the large real exchange rate depreciation needed to have a significant impact on the economy.

—Chile's growth potential likely gained from its high degree of trade integration. Numerous empirical studies indicate that countries with open trade regimes have grown more quickly than those with a lower degree of international integration.[3]

• *Institutional arrangements were set to create a more certain macroeconomic environment.* Sound economic policies and reforms have been carried out within an incentive-based institutional framework to avoid their reversal when they become inconvenient or costly in the short run. The institutional arrangements, inter alia, have reduced the incentives problem that elsewhere have led to a chronic lack of fiscal discipline, complex and distorted trade policies, and runaway moral hazard in the financial system.

Four Thematic Areas of This Paper

With a view to enhancing our understanding of the Chilean experience—including both accomplishments and areas for potential improvement—the contributions of this paper are grouped in four thematic areas: the macroeconomic and institutional framework; recent developments in financial markets; an assessment of the domestic position of the public sector and the country's external position; and the role of

exports in economic growth. While recognizing that one country's route to success is not fully transferable to other emerging market economies, the paper presents what may be a useful reference on the Chilean experience in these four areas.

Macroeconomic and Institutional Framework

A sizable literature has documented Chile's sound economic policies over the last decade, but less attention has been given to the factors behind the adoption and continuation of such policies.[4] Section II of this paper takes a long view of Chile's reform experience and considers the role played by institutional factors in Chile's economic policies and performance. It presents a deeper view of the Chilean experience by considering how institutional arrangements may have helped policymakers to identify and implement, and then maintain, sound policies.

The review of Chile's institutions focuses on four policy objectives which make up the core areas of IMF work and where it is widely acknowledged that Chile has been particularly strong: sustaining fiscal policy discipline; policies to maintain price stability; policies that promote financial stability; and an open and stable trade policy regime. Among the numerous institutional arrangements discussed, the constitutional features that have promoted fiscal discipline—including budget process rules and the tight constraints on subnational governments—and effective central bank independence have been especially important.

In recent years, and building on its institutional foundations, Chile has refined its macroeconomic policy framework. Having exited its exchange rate band arrangement without a crisis, Chile opted for a floating exchange rate system. In addition, the country gradually settled into a full-fledged inflation-targeting framework and a fiscal rule.

Section III of the paper describes the main elements of the inflation-targeting framework in Chile, which currently consists of (1) a prespecified continuous inflation target band; (2) a preannounced "policy horizon"; and (3) timely communication of the authorities' inflation forecast, the rationale for their policy decisions, and the reasons for any temporary deviations from the inflation target. The paper argues that an important supplement to this framework is the absence of an exchange rate target. Chile's exchange rate policy calls for zero exchange intervention, with the possibility of intervention only under exceptional circumstances. When intervention does take place, the authorities announce the event, reveal

---

[3]For example, see Dollar and Kraay (2003).

[4]For example, see Schmidt-Hebbel (1999) and the references therein.

the amount of the intervention, and most importantly do not target a specific exchange rate.

Section III also explains the mechanics of the fiscal rule. This mechanism has increased transparency and accountability by defining a specific medium-term fiscal policy path that removes policy discretion while not suppressing automatic stabilizers. The use of expert panels to determine cyclical adjustments to meet the rule has enhanced transparency and credibility.

Recent Developments in Financial Markets

The privatization of pension funds' management, capital market reforms, and macroeconomic stability have worked to deepen capital markets in Chile.

Section IV reviews the development of domestic capital markets and corporate financing in recent years and draws on remaining policy challenges going forward. The analysis underscores the role of macroeconomic policies and structural reforms as the driving factors underpinning the development of local securities markets in the 1990s. The presence of a well-developed and large institutional investor base has also played a fundamental role as a stable and growing source of domestic finance. While equity markets expanded rapidly in the early 1990s, the domestic corporate bond market has experienced a remarkable resurgence since 2000 as large corporate firms, in particular, sought to time the market following the sharp drop in domestic interest rates.

Despite this progress, the future development of domestic capital markets faces key challenges related to the low liquidity in equity and corporate bond markets and the high degree of ownership and investor concentration. Recent changes in financial regulation and legislation have sought to address concerns about the relative depth of capital markets and effectiveness of corporate governance while improving capital market regulation. Policymakers have thus been actively working to improve financial market infrastructure, seeking to establish appropriate incentives to harness market discipline and self-regulation. As demonstrated by the recent reforms, the authorities have underscored the role of bridging missing markets, promoting liquidity and transparency, and providing incentives to wider access to investment resources.

The banking system has been another key player in the allocation of credit to the private sector. For the last twenty years, the Chilean banking system has had access to fairly strong technology to evaluate consumers' creditworthiness. And since the mid-1980s, it has enjoyed a reputation for stability and strength, while continuing to evolve.

Section V provides an update on the Chilean banking system, indicating that it continues to remain robust, and also highlighting structural features and recent developments. In particular, the section documents the recent "Inverlink" case, in which a corrupt private financial company fell, after having sold stolen government securities to the market. This case originated outside of, but nevertheless had repercussions for, the banking system. The section discusses the responses of the authorities to this episode, both the immediate actions to address liquidity needs, as well as forward-looking measures to improve financial security. It also describes key factors behind the active role played by banks in the allocation of credit to the private sector.

The Domestic Financial Position of the Public Sector and the Country's External Financial Position

The assessment of the public sector finances is favorable. Since risky balance sheet structures have been avoided, exposure to currency and interest rate risks is limited. The analysis in Section VI suggests that as long as the government's fiscal structural balance target continues to be met, the public finances will remain sustainable.

Section VI makes use of newly available balance sheet data on the debt and financial assets of the Chilean public sector. Much of the analysis centers on the finances of the central government. Taking into account the government's structural balance target, it is difficult to see debt sustainability problems emerging, as long as this target is met (or fiscal policy otherwise remains restrained). The section also examines the central bank's balance sheet, including its tendency to run a modest operational deficit. It notes the considerable strength of the central bank in terms of foreign exchange and liquidity positions. Though the bank's deficit has been fairly stable and has not interfered with its monetary policy objectives, the section suggests some steps, including a capital injection from the government, that could be taken to improve its financial position. The situation of the public enterprises appears sound, especially in light of their overall profitability and limited debt.

An assessment of the country's external financial position also requires a close look at the external position of the corporate sector, including the relationship with parent companies. An important source of vulnerability for many countries is their external financial position. How resilient a country is to external liquidity squeezes on the balance of payments will determine, in many instances, whether a country encounters a bump on the road or a full-fledged crisis.

Section VII assesses Chile's external position, integrating information on the country's international investment position and structure of external debt. The analysis considers the possibility of an external liquidity shock on the balance of payments while testing for potential solvency problems. The approach combines the standard IMF debt sustainability analysis framework and alternative tests using data on Chile's international investment position. The analysis focuses on (1) the external debt dynamics; (2) the sensitivity of gross external financing requirements to specific shocks; and (3) the implications of Chile's international investment position for external vulnerability.

The analysis underscores the strength of Chile's aggregate external position. In a standard debt sustainability framework, various hypothetical shocks would lead to a substantial, though temporary, increase in the external debt-to-GDP ratio. However, the risks of these standardized shocks seem remote, given the strength of Chile's current policy framework. Liquidity problems are not expected given the country's significant liquid foreign assets, held by both the public and private sectors. Chile's large foreign asset–liability structure is another source of strength. The large foreign direct investment in Chile helps explain the observation that foreign-owned Chilean resident firms hold more than half of Chile's total external debt. Sensitivity analysis using the net international investment position also shows the dampening effects of the large direct investment on the country's aggregate net liability.

Export Specialization and Economic Growth

Not all countries have benefited equally from globalization. Furthermore, there is some economic literature suggesting a negative relationship between natural resource exports and long-term growth. Chile is well known for its early, often unilateral, aggressive trade liberalization efforts. Therefore it is worth looking into Chile's experience.

Section VIII suggests that Chile has benefited from increased integration with the global economy. Chile's export sector has promoted competitiveness, positive spillovers, and economic growth. The section's conclusions are based on the analysis of the role, past and prospective, of exports in the growth of the Chilean economy with a focus on export specialization: in the Chilean case, following comparative advantage often has meant exporting goods that are natural resource based. The section offers a critical assessment of the notion that such exports are necessarily stagnant and have a negative impact on a country's rate of growth. In the case of Chile, these exports have been associated with positive spillovers leading to the creation of new products, emphasizing the need to promote human capital accumulation in order to take advantage of these spillovers, increase productivity, and continue diversifying the Chilean export basket.

References

Calvo, G., and C. Reinhart, 2000, "When Capital Inflows Suddenly Stop: Consequences and Policy Options," in *Reforming the International Monetary and Financial System,* ed. by P. Kenen and A. Swoboda (Washington: International Monetary Fund).

Dollar, D., and A. Kraay, 2003, "Institutions, Trade, and Growth," *Journal of Monetary Economics*, Vol. 50, No. 1 (January), pp. 133–65.

Massad, C., 2003, "The Chilean Experience from the 1990s," CSIS Report (Washington: Center for Strategic and International Studies).

Schmidt-Hebbel, K., 1999, "Chile's Takeoff: Facts, Challenges, Lessons," in *Chile, Recent Policy Lessons and Emerging Challenges,* ed. by G. Perry and D. Leipziger (Washington: World Bank).

II   The Role of Institutions in Chile

Marco A. Espinosa-Vega and Steven Phillips

This section considers the role played by institutional factors in Chile's economic policies and performance. Chile's successful economic performance is well documented, and its economic policy reforms are generally accepted as key to that performance. Less attention has been given, however, to the role played by institutions in this success, either in terms of their direct effects on economic performance or in the establishment of good economic policies.

This section seeks to gain a deeper view of the Chilean experience by considering the role institutional factors have played in *sustaining good policies* over time. A key motivating idea is that sustaining policy reforms often requires countering negative incentives that had been responsible for previous unsound policies.

The approach taken here differs from most recent applied studies on institutions.[1] Much of this literature looks at the association of institutions with outcomes for income and growth, not necessarily considering the role of policies (see Box 2.1). In contrast, the focus of this paper is policy based, taking into account the public sector decision process and the political economy underlying policy actions. Also, while much of the recent empirical literature statistically analyzes differences across countries in perceptions and assessments of institutional quality, it does not usually analyze differences over time. The "narrative approach" used here does not permit statistical analysis, but it does give a closer view of one country, and some historical perspective on how its institutions emerged and how they helped change—or maintain—policies over time.

The Chilean case is particularly instructive partly because the country has not always been so successful.[2] Its strong economic performance is still relatively recent—starting in the mid-1980s—and has been tested by episodes of financial crisis that hit the East Asian tigers and other emerging market economies in 1997–98, as well as some of Chile's neighbors in 2001–02.

This review of Chile's institutions is selective, looking at those that have been significant in four policy areas in which Chile is widely agreed to be particularly strong:

- Fiscal policy discipline;

- Policies to maintain price stability;

- Banking policies to promote financial stability; and

- An open trade policy regime.

Of course, not every aspect of Chile's economic policy record can be traced clearly to some institutional arrangement. Other factors—such as consensus on economic issues, the technical expertise or benevolence of policymakers, or cultural factors more generally—may also play a role, but these are beyond the scope of this section.

This section first looks at the political rules of the game: aspects of Chile's constitution and political framework relevant for economic policy outcomes. Chile's system has a number of characteristics that cross-country studies have found to be associated with sound policies.

Next, the role of institutions in each of the four broad areas highlighted above is examined, namely, fiscal discipline, price stability, banking stability, and trade policy. For each area, note is first made of the problems any country may face in choosing, implementing, and sustaining good policies, and then the question of how these problems have been addressed (or not) by institutional arrangements in Chile is examined. Some pending issues and possible areas for future institutional development are also discussed.

---

[1]IMF (2003a) offers a recent survey of this burgeoning literature.

[2]Over the period 1940–70, Chile was in many ways typical of much of Latin America, in following an import-substitution strategy, giving a heavy role to the state in the economy more generally, rationing foreign exchange, and experiencing high and unstable inflation. Moreover, after major reforms of this old regime began in the 1970s, Chile exemplified a problem that has been

familiar elsewhere, with its severe financial crisis of the early 1980s.

Box 2.1. Some Other Research Referring to Chilean Institutions

Recent empirical research on the influence of institutions focuses on relating proxies for institutions to countries' level of income or growth rate. Proxies for public institutions can for example refer to the quality of governance, the extent of legal protection of private property, and limits placed on political leaders (see IMF, 2003a, for a fuller discussion). The focus of this literature is on cross-country differences, since institutional indicators for a given country may not change much, even over long periods.

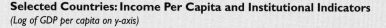

Selected Countries: Income Per Capita and Institutional Indicators
(Log of GDP per capita on y-axis)

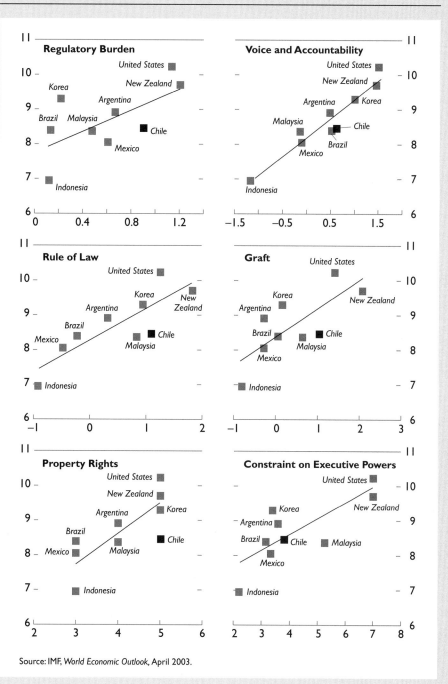

Source: IMF, *World Economic Outlook*, April 2003.

Box 2.1 *(concluded)*

The hope is to gain insight into the potential rewards to improvements in institutional quality. For example, in studying a sample of Latin American countries, Calderón and Schmidt-Hebbel (2003) find that a one-standard-deviation increase in their index of governance is on average associated with a 0.75 percent increase in the growth rate. IMF (2003a) finds that an increase of one standard deviation in an aggregate measure of governance seems to reduce output volatility by over one-fourth on average. That study also finds that the countries with the weakest institutions would benefit the most from an improvement of their public institutions.

The accompanying figure gives a sense of how Chile fits into such analyses. It uses data from IMF (2003a) for Chile, a group of Latin American and East Asian economies, New Zealand, and the United States, plotting per capita income against each of six indicators of institutions. Chile's indicators compare favorably to those of the other emerging market economies, but are not as strong as those of New Zealand or the United States. Interestingly, the Chilean data point tends to lie below the fitted lines also shown in the figure, signifying that Chilean institutions are somewhat better than would be expected given the country's income level, but also that income is less than would be expected given the quality of the country's institutions.

The final subsection offers some closing observations. These include identifying some additional areas in which institutional arrangements may have played a significant role in Chile in the past, and some which may be particularly important looking forward.

Political Rules of the Game: The Constitution and Political Framework

This section presents selected aspects of the political framework, especially Chile's constitution, that have significance for economic policies and institutions. This is essential background, for in a basic sense the political framework has to underlie all Chilean institutions: either the political framework gave rise to these or at the minimum allowed their development.

Aspects and Origins of Chile's Constitution

Chile's current constitution is still often referred to as the "1980 constitution," and indeed the military government that took power in 1973 had a key role in its development. Yet the current constitution can also be seen as a modified version of the 1925 constitution.

Some of the most significant aspects of the constitution, relating to the budget process, were introduced in 1970, before the period of military rule, and subsequently retained in the 1980 constitution. While the 1925 constitution had given the executive ample powers in many areas, governments had difficulty negotiating and obtaining approval of budgets in a timely and effective way; the reforms introduced in 1970 have "greatly limited the scope for vested interests to lobby on fiscal affairs" (Foxley, 2003; and Foxley and Sapelli, 1999). As explained in the section "Fiscal Discipline: The Role of Institutions,"

power in the process of determining the budget was tilted strongly toward the executive.

Although the 1980 constitution took a step toward insulating monetary policy from political pressures, the charter of an independent central bank was established constitutionally only in 1989. The 1980 constitution prohibited the central bank from purchasing government securities, but left the bank still vulnerable to government pressure and to private sector demands for direct credit. Independence came with the 1989 Basic Constitutional Act of the Central Bank (discussed in the section "Financial Stability: The Chilean Approach to Banking Supervision, Regulation, and Safety Net"). This special law has a constitutional character, and any amendments to it would require a three-fifths majority in congress.

The Electoral System

The electoral system established by the constitution has a number of aspects likely to influence economic policy outcomes, including the following:

- "Presidentialist," in that the country's president is elected in a direct vote, at fixed intervals of six years, and does not require congressional support to remain in office;

- Majoritarian, rather than proportional, determination of congressional representation; and

- Electoral rules for congressional seats, which create strong incentives for individual political parties to join coalitions.[3] Most likely reflecting such incentives, the result since the return to democ-

---

[3]Many systems of voting rules grant an extra degree of representation to an election's first-place finisher, and this is true in Chile also. What distinguishes the Chilean system is that there is also an extra reward, in terms of representation, to finishing in second place (as opposed to coming in third). This feature of the

racy has been two large voting blocs, which so far have proven stable. Though at least six political parties of significant size continue to exist, in many ways Chilean politics now approximates a two-party system.

A cross-country empirical literature has found such features to be associated with greater fiscal policy discipline.[4] As emphasized by Foxley and Sapelli (1999), the incentives in Chile to form coalitions give reasons for individual political parties to moderate their particular demands in favor of the common interest. By avoiding political polarization and governmental instability, incentives for policymakers to behave myopically have been reduced. While the country's president is limited to serving one term, incentives to pursue only short-term gains are put in check by the term's being relatively long, as well as by rules on contracting debt with maturity extending beyond the president's term.

In the area of establishing the annual budget law, the Chilean system assures a prompt resolution, achieving this by giving a critical advantage to the executive over the legislature. In contrast, in other economic policy areas requiring passage of a law, the system is not designed for speed, but rather building consensus. In that sense, the system tends to favor policy stability, something that may give confidence to private agents to make long-term investments.

Fiscal Discipline: The Role of Institutions

We first note the problems in sustaining fiscal discipline in any country and then look at how these have been addressed by institutional arrangements in Chile. The focus is on the "big picture" institutions and those factors of direct relevance to maintaining fiscal discipline over time (essentially, safeguarding the balance sheet of the public sector).[5] We close by surveying some pending fiscal policy issues in Chile.

Inherent Challenges to Fiscal Discipline

In the fiscal area, we focus on institutions relevant to countering the following potential problems and threats to fiscal discipline:

- *The common pool problem.* Subnational governments with inadequate budget constraints are a prominent example;[6] more generally, any situation in which a lack of centralized budget decision making allows particular groups to lobby for public sector actions to their own benefit, without internalizing the associated costs.

- *Various intertemporal problems.* These include time inconsistency issues and the resulting "deficit bias." Another concern is the so-called myopia of policymakers without adequate incentives to be concerned with the future implications of their decisions (often attributed to situations of very frequent political turnover, or to the fact that future generations lack political representation).

Left unchecked, these problems are likely to result in a weak public sector balance sheet: a high level of public debt (up to the limits of market tolerance), but also a risky structure of liabilities, emphasizing forms of debt that are seemingly cheap from a short-term perspective, but carry high rollover, interest rate, and exchange rate risk.

Chilean Approaches to Maintaining Fiscal Discipline: Budget Constraints

The problem of indiscipline by subnational governments has been kept to a minimum in Chile by the simple but tough approach of prohibiting subnational governments from borrowing. More precisely, subnational governments are prohibited from issuing or contracting financial debt unless a specific authorizing law is passed, which so far has never happened.[7] Potential budget constraint problems, then, are limited to arrears that may be run with suppliers (in turn, kept in check by the threat of legal action and suppliers' ability to suspend deliveries). In recent years, the central government has sought to tie its own hands, to credibly commit not to favor arrears with transfers to local governments, using annual budget laws.

---

voting rules gives political parties incentives to form coalitions, and thus to sacrifice some of their special interests in the process.

[4]An empirical literature has found that large government debt and deficits are more common in countries with proportional rather than majoritarian representation, coalition governments and frequent turnover, and lenient rather than strict budget processes. Many such studies have focused on industrial countries (for a review, see Annett, 2002), but Alesina and others (1999) and Stein and others (1999) also found similar results for Latin American countries.

[5]That is, we do not survey fiscal policy issues in Chile, such as questions of the efficiency of public expenditure and taxation. Nor do we cover all the arrangements that may—or may not—contribute to fiscal discipline (e.g., a good tax administration, in the absence of the right budget incentives, might not be associated with fiscal discipline).

---

[6]Jones, Sanguinetti, and Tommaso (2000) analyze problems of the Argentine case.

[7]Municipalities do not have to run continuously balanced budgets, as they have the ability to accumulate assets and subsequently draw these down as needed. Taken as a group, however, municipal governments' annual overall balance in practice has stayed very close to balance.

Credibility of the budget constraint on subnational governments is supported by the relatively small size of any one such government. In Chile, "subnational governments" refer to "municipalities," rather than to a small number of relatively large provinces or regions.[8] Municipalities therefore tend not to be "too big to fail."

For the central government, arrangements that harden its budget constraint include:

- Government borrowing is subject to congressional approval;

- Public sector borrowing from the central bank is prohibited, while independence of the central bank insulates it from potential government pressure to finance quasi-fiscal expenditure;

- The current government's innovative target for its structural balance—discussed below—also focuses attention on the government's intertemporal budget constraint.

Budget Process

The budget process in Chile contains several features likely to help counter the common pool problem, and that have been found in cross-country empirical studies to be associated with greater fiscal discipline. The budget process is dominated by the executive branch rather than the legislature, and by the finance ministry rather than spending ministries. Budget reforms introduced in 1970 and retained in the 1980 constitution greatly limit the scope for particular interests to lobby on fiscal affairs. Thus only the executive can initiate fiscal measures, and there is a 60-day limit on congress' budget approval process. If after 60 days congress has not been able to agree among itself, and with the government, on a modification of the government's proposed budget law, then the *government's initial budget proposal automatically becomes law*.

Responding Appropriately to Shocks

Chile is a significant exporter of copper, and since the government is owner of a large copper producer, government receipts are sensitive to variations in world prices. While governments of some countries have stumbled over managing such volatility in their own export earnings—often re-

---

[8]As part of a decentralization effort, regional governments do exist for each of Chile's 13 regions. However, these are not separate governments in the usual sense: they are not constituted via regional elections, their revenue and financing powers are quite limited, and their expenditures are part of a unified central government budget.

lated to oil exports—Chile has a number of strategies that seem to have helped. First, the government has not insisted on owning all production of the commodity in question, and so has reduced the income volatility it faces. A second strategy involves the Copper Stabilization Fund (CSF), a mechanism established in law. This requires that the government make deposits corresponding to the "excess" income received during periods of higher copper prices and make withdrawals from the CSF during times of lower prices. A third strategy is the recent introduction of a target for the government's structural balance, which makes an adjustment for copper price variations.

Some authors consider that the CSF has been a useful device, in particular by helping the government increase its saving during the copper boom years around the mid-1990s. Empirically, Davis and others (2001) found that government expenditure has been less tightly correlated with commodity revenue in Chile than elsewhere. However, the mechanism for this apparent success is not clear, since the design of the CSF does not strictly constrain government spending: in principle, the government could simply borrow to replace the funds deposited into the CSF. Possibly, the CSF was instead useful through its special accounting rules, which allowed the government to avoid showing a surplus and therefore reduced political pressure for additional spending.

The Structural Balance Target: An Institution in Development?

The government that took office in early 2000 committed itself to an ongoing target for its structural balance, a significant innovation with the potential to counter some of the most difficult problems in maintaining fiscal discipline. Under this informal rule, the government prepares each year's budget to be consistent with holding steady the level of its structural balance (see Section III). This new practice:

- Allows tight accountability, yet without need to suppress automatic stabilizers.

- Makes very transparent the government's budget constraint: any proposal for new expenditure or tax cuts requires an immediate offsetting policy action.

- Provides a longer-term goal for fiscal policy, breaking away from year-at-a-time fiscal decision making. This ties the government's hands against problems such as election cycle spending.

- Provides a systematic approach to fiscal policy's response to shocks, eliminating room for slippery decisions of whether to adjust policy now or "later."

- Ensures attention to the government's intertemporal budget constraint (all but ruling out problems of debt dynamics and sustainability; see Section VII).

The practice of targeting a steady structural balance—if maintained—should thus go a long way in avoiding time inconsistency problems and deficit bias of fiscal policy.

Pending Issues in Fiscal Policy Institutions

We have seen that the institutional framework in Chile has important features that tend to promote fiscal discipline, and certainly the record of sustained discipline in Chile is impressive. Still, it is possible to identify some pending institutional issues:

- *Institutionalizing fiscal transparency.* Chile was able to sustain fiscal discipline over the years without a particularly high level of fiscal transparency; indeed, many of Chile's current strength in terms of transparency are steps taken just in the last few years.[9] Nevertheless, transparency may help sustain fiscal discipline in the future, and it could be useful to formally institutionalize many of the recent improvements (many being steps first taken on an ad hoc basis). This process seems to be under way.

- *Institutionalization of the structural balance target?* Although this new framework represents a significant advance, it has no legal or permanent status, and some of its potential advantages may not be realized if there is doubt that the policy will be sustained. While the commitment of the current government may well be credible, it cannot extend beyond the government's term. It may be worth considering more formally institutionalizing at least some aspects of the structural balance target.

- *Too much reliance on a benevolent executive?* Following the literature, we have emphasized the advantages of the dominance of the executive in Chile's budget process. In principle, this reliance could someday backfire, but the remedy is unclear. Assurances seem to come not from institutional arrangements but rather from the roles of political consensus and political accountability, joined in recent years by the increased transparency of fiscal policy.

---

[9]See IMF (2003c).

The Quest for Price Stability: The Role of Institutional Arrangements

Chile has achieved price stability: low and stable inflation. Here we consider the role institutional arrangements related to monetary policy—for example, central bank independence—have played in this success. However, a recurring theme is that fiscal discipline played a key role in achieving price stability.

Monetary policy frameworks or rules, or exchange rate regimes, in some cases can be seen not only as policies but also as institutional arrangements that may—or may not—promote price stability. We conclude that Chile's inflation-targeting framework is contributing substantively to price stability, and moreover that this framework is developing a sort of informal institutional status. On the other hand, we argue that the various exchange rate regime choices of Chile's past worked, in several instances, as a distraction from the price stability goal.

In any country, a number of potential obstacles and incentive problems need to be countered in order to achieve price stability. These include, in various combinations: lack of independence of the central bank, so-called fiscal dominance, unclear mandates, inconsistent policy objectives, or, more generally, time inconsitency problems. As have other countries, Chile struggled with most of these classic problems at one time or other. In this section, we note some of these past difficulties as well as more recent successes.

The Independence and Mandate of the Central Bank

A Chilean institution that enjoys wide credit for contributing to price stability is the independence of the central bank, with its clear mandate to promote price stability.

The case for central bank independence is well developed in the literature. Arguments such as those summarized in Box 2.2 have led a number of countries to institutionalize the independence of the central bank and charge it with price stability.

Several researchers, including Cukierman (1992) and Alesina and Summers (1993), have constructed indexes to measure central bank independence. In general, they have found a relationship between measures of independence and lower inflation, in samples consisting mostly of developed economies.

Until recently, empirical work had found little evidence of a relationship between independence of the central bank and good inflation performance for Latin America. Recently, Gutierrez (2003) suggests this is due to a disconnect between what is stated in central bank charters and their actual degree of in-

---

Box 2.2. Central Bank Independence

To achieve price stability, many governments have turned their attention to the design of institutions such as an independent central bank charged with price stability. Inflation targeting has been a hallmark of monetary policymaking in Chile since 1990, but in the last several years it has taken a more advanced form, known as an inflation-targeting framework.

In their classic work, "Some Unpleasant Monetarist Arithmetic," Sargent and Wallace (1985) showed how monetary policy and fiscal policy interact so that the effects of changes in monetary policy may depend on the response of fiscal policy. In their analysis, the inflationary implications of a change in monetary policy depend critically on how the government manages its debt. For example, a dominant and undisciplined fiscal policy could result in either an explosive government debt path or, if the monetary authority "blinked," in high monetization of the ever-growing government debt and consequently high inflation down the road—and possibly in the short run.

A corollary to the Sargent and Wallace argument is that under some conditions, monetary policy could im-

pose discipline on fiscal policy. If there were no question about the monetary policy commitment to low and stable inflation—if the monetary authority "moved first," and did not or, better yet, could not "blink"—such a commitment could impose discipline on fiscal policy. Knowing that its debt would never be monetized, the fiscal authority would face two choices: continue along an explosive debt path or submit to discipline. The second choice would be more likely because there is a limit to how much government debt can be absorbed by the market.

Another important reason for the establishment of an independent central bank is trying to address a monetary authority's time inconsistency problem. Barro and Gordon (1983) present an extension of Kydland and Prescott's (1977) seminal work on a typical government's time inconsistency problem. Barro and Gordon showed that even a well-intentioned central bank may be tempted to deviate from the long-term optimum, with significant adverse inflationary consequences. An independent central bank may be able to focus on a longer time horizon and thus resist temporary pressures to give in to monetization.

---

dependence. Gutierrez constructs an index for Latin American countries that only considers what the constitution states about the central bank and ignores the central bank charter. The way the autonomy of the Central Bank of Chile is embedded in the constitution leads Gutierrez to rank Chile as third (in a sample of 25 countries) in this refined index of central bank independence. She also finds a relationship in her sample between her measure of central bank independence and low inflation.

Indeed, Chile's 1980 constitution (Article 97, Chapter XII) granted constitutional status to the existence of an autonomous central bank, defining the bank as a *technical entity with its own equity capital*. Article 98 states that the central bank may only carry out operations with financial institutions in the public or private sector. The constitution *specifically prohibited the central bank from granting guarantees or acquiring documents issued by the state, its agencies or companies.*

Only in 1989, however, did the central bank achieve full independence. Only then were the bank's specific mandate, organization, powers, responsibilities, accountability, and relationships with the finance ministry instituted. The organization and functions of . the bank were specified in the 1989 Basic Constitutional Act of the Central Bank of Chile.[10]

The 1989 Basic Act charged the central bank with price stability and the normal functioning of the payments system. To achieve this, the bank was granted broad regulatory powers over monetary, credit, financial, and foreign exchange activity.

- To solidify the independence of the central bank, the Basic Act established the selection criteria and composition of its board. The board consists of five members, nominated by the president and ratified by the senate. Terms are 10 years, with one member's term ending every 2 years. The president names one of the board members as president of the central bank, for a 5-year term.

- The Basic Act establishes clear accountability criteria. The central bank is required to inform the senate and the president of the norms it dictates. The central bank is also obligated to testify before congress twice a year.

- The Basic Act also institutes the relationship between the central bank and the finance ministry. In particular, the law states that the finance minister can attend and speak at board meetings, but cannot vote. (If the board does not vote unanimously on an issue, the minister of finance can suspend the application of the board's decisions, though only for a maximum of 15 days.)

---

[10]*Ley Orgánica Constitucional del Banco Central de Chile.*

Did an Independent Central Bank Force Fiscal Discipline?

An important fact to highlight along Chile's disinflationary journey was a switch in the role of the central bank. During some periods prior to 1989, the central bank functioned as a virtual agency of the treasury. Morandé (2001, p. 1), for example, states: "As in many other countries, fiscal policy became extremely expansive and eventually irresponsible... Monetary policy was almost always an expression of fiscal needs; high and volatile inflation was an unsurprising outcome."

In 1989, the full-fledged autonomy of the central bank came into existence coinciding with two significant developments in Chile. After 1989 the government showed remarkable fiscal discipline in the sense of a dramatic strengthening of its balance sheet. Coupled with strong rates of output growth, fiscal discipline resulted in a smooth decline of the consolidated debt to GDP ratio. At the same time, the country also initiated its convergence to price stability (Figure 2.1). Possibly, the full-fledged independence of the central bank helped prompt fiscal discipline and in that way the attainment of price stability, as suggested by the theories described in Box 2.2. Of course, this association is only suggestive, and it is quite possible that the fiscal authority was convinced on its own of the need for fiscal discipline, and not only as a means to price stability.[11]

Central Bank Independence: Helpful but Not Enough for Price Stability?

Recently, a number of authors (Sims (2003), Cochrane (2001), and Woodford (2001)) have revisited the idea that the institution of an independent central bank is enough to guarantee price stability. They show that the central bank could be independent, indeed never monetizing government debt, yet bursts of inflation could still occur in response to sharp accumulation of government debt. This theory would suggest that although helpful, central bank independence may not be enough to assure price stability; it may be a good idea to also institute limits to the debt issuance on the part of the fiscal authority or a rule limiting the budget deficit.

Catao and Terrones (2003) carry out an empirical assessment of theories suggesting the importance

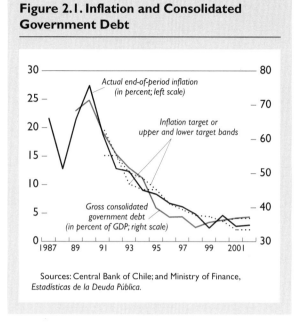

Figure 2.1. Inflation and Consolidated Government Debt

Actual end-of-period inflation (in percent; left scale)

Inflation target or upper and lower target bands

Gross consolidated government debt (in percent of GDP; right scale)

Sources: Central Bank of Chile; and Ministry of Finance, *Estadísticas de la Deuda Pública.*

of fiscal factors in the determination of a country's inflation rate. They show that the size of fiscal deficits does matter, even for countries with moderate inflation. Although their analysis does not discriminate between the theories in Box 2.2 or the most recent developments of the fiscal theory of the price level, their finding reinforces the view that fiscal factors matter for price stability.

Inflation Targeting: An Emerging Informal Institution

Credit for Chile's price stability is also due to the practice of inflation targeting, which itself recently has taken on institutional qualities.

Some form of inflation targeting has been a hallmark of monetary policymaking in Chile since 1990, but in the last several years it has taken a more advanced form, known as an "inflation-targeting framework" (see Section III). The question is whether inflation targeting has played a substantive role in achieving and maintaining price stability or whether it has been mainly an operational change.[12]

[11]In his own account of his experience as Chile's Minister of Finance in the early 1990s, Foxley (2003) reports that this was the case.

[12]For a comprehensive analysis of the inflation-targeting experience in Chile and elsewhere, see the conference proceedings of the Central Bank of Chile (2000).

From 1990 to 1999, inflation targeting was not full-fledged.[13] The target sometimes consisted of announcing an upper bound for next year's inflation and sometimes of announcing a band. Each year's announced target was lower than the previous one, but the level of the target was announced only one year at a time. The target was not continuous but rather referred to end-year outcomes, there was no clear policy horizon, and the inflation objective rested uneasily with the exchange rate target band in place at the same time. That said, this period did see an important, if gradual, decline in Chile's rate of inflation.

Following 1999, by which time the central bank had achieved its desired steady-state inflation rate and dropped the exchange rate target band, inflation targeting in Chile was developed into a full-fledged framework, consisting of a preannounced band, a well-understood measure of inflation, and an announced policy horizon.[14]

The move to full-fledged inflation targeting seems more than a change in operational style. Corbo and Schmidt-Hebbel (2001) and Schmidt-Hebbel and Tapia (2002) argue that inflation targeting also has played a substantive role by anchoring expectations and strengthening the credibility of monetary policy and official inflation forecasts. Moreover, the central bank's announcement of an explicit inflation target is potentially a strong commitment and verification device. Consistent with that interpretation of the Chilean experience, Orphanides and Williams (2002) present a theoretical analysis in which a policy of emphasizing price stability as an operational policy objective, and the periodic communication of a central bank's inflation objectives, works to anchor inflation expectations, in turn facilitating price stability. In the Chilean case, by choosing a well-known price index and a policy horizon that allows for standard lag effects,[15] inflation targeting may generate greater public understanding of the central bank's objectives, hence increasing the credibility of the framework.

The track record under inflation targeting has been favorable. Actual inflation has generally remained inside the target band. Indicators of inflation expectations also have been consistent with the inflation target (see Section III).

Exchange Rate Arrangements: Help or Hindrance in the Journey to Price Stability?

Fixed exchange rate schemes are sometimes considered as institutional arrangements to attain price stability. However, no such supporting role is found in Chile's modern experience. The last attempt to use the exchange rate as a nominal anchor resulted in a *temporary* decline in inflation before ending in failure in 1982.[16]

Subsequently, a kind of hybrid, more ad hoc exchange rate regime, sometimes called a managed float, was pursued from 1985 to 1999, which included an exchange rate band. However, this policy was not used to help the disinflation objective being pursued during the 1990s: rather than an effort to limit depreciation of the peso and thereby establish a nominal anchor, during much of the 1990s it involved an active effort to avoid or slow down peso appreciation.[17] Significant purchases of foreign exchange during this period required a costly sterilization process, aimed to counteract inflationary consequences of pursuing the exchange rate objective.[18]

The floating exchange rate regime in place since 1999 is fully compatible with the goal of price stability. The absence of an exchange rate objective allows the central bank more room to pursue its inflation objective, with greater focus.

Pending Issues and Questions

In light of Chile's success in achieving price stability, there certainly is no presumption that important changes in institutional arrangements are needed. However, a few points could be considered:

---

[13]As Morandé (2001, p. 5) notes, inflation targeting was adopted in 1990 "in part by accident, in part out of necessity, in part for lack of alternatives, and in part in reflection of a longer-run view of monetary policy. The move was accidental in that the recently inaugurated independent Central Bank was required by its charter to present a report to Congress each September, outlining the prospects for the economy for the following calendar year (in particular with regard to inflation. . .). A target for inflation fit naturally with the price stabilization goal established in that charter. . . .The inflation projection was treated as a target."

[14]The band centered at 3 percent with a lower bound of 2 percent and an upper bound of 4 percent. The targeted measure of inflation has been in percentage changes in the consumer price index. Recognizing that monetary policy affects inflation with a long lag, the central bank's policy horizon was specified to be from 12 to 24 months. See also Section III.

[15]Schmidt-Hebbel and Tapia (2002) emphasize also that the announced policy horizon allows constrained discretion.

[16]From 1979 to 1982, the country adopted a hard peg meant to play the role of a nominal anchor by linking domestic inflation to the U.S. inflation. The strategy worked—until losses of official reserves prompted devaluation in 1982, associated with a banking crisis, a burst of inflation, and severe recession.

[17]According to Morandé and Tapia (2002, p. 2), throughout some of the managed float years, "the concern was not placed in the exchange rate as the anchor to lower inflation. . . , but as an instrument to sustain a depreciated real exchange rate that would boost exports."

[18]Relatedly, measures to limit capital inflows were also applied, but ended in 1998.

- If inflation targeting contributes importantly to price stability, this might suggest formally institutionalizing the practice, as a way to ensure its continuance. Currently, the framework is implemented at the discretion of the central bank's board. However, in the absence of any clear threat to maintaining the best aspects of inflation targeting, any legal changes might be unnecessary (and not worth the possible risks inherent in opening up the central bank law for political discussion).

- More practically, the inflation-targeting framework could be enhanced by making more explicit the model and assumptions used in the inflation-targeting framework, in particular the methods used to forecast inflation over the horizon used to evaluate the monetary stance. Indeed, the central bank plans to do this soon.

- As noted earlier, Chile's constitution defines the central bank as an autonomous entity "with its own capital." However, the central bank's tendency to run an operational deficit (see Section VII) could—if sustained—undermine the bank's capital base. A solution to this situation would be for the government to recapitalize the central bank, a move that would also increase transparency of *fiscal* policy and that would tend to safeguard public confidence in the future independence of the central bank.

Financial Stability: The Chilean Approach to Banking Supervision, Regulation, and Safety Net

This subsection considers whether Chile's banking regulatory and safety net institutions have been established to maintain stability. To a large degree this comes down to countering the problem of moral hazard in banking, by providing appropriate incentives to banking system participants, both banks and depositors. Research has shown (e.g., Barth and others (2002) and Boyd and Rolnick (1988)) that a key condition for bank stability is for depositors and banks to be motivated to act as if a government bailout would be an event both very rare and extremely costly for them.

To understand the origin of Chile's current banking supervision, regulation, and safety net institutions, mostly based in the banking law of 1986, it is useful to start with an overview of the banking crisis of 1982–84. We then review the characteristics of sound banking policy institutions, and document the considerable extent to which the Chilean approach is consistent with these.

The Banking Crisis of 1982–84: Setting the Stage for Reform

The consensus view (e.g., de la Cuadra and Valdes, 1992) of this banking crisis is that external shocks triggered a chain of events that revealed underlying vulnerabilities. These included connected lending, overly generous implicit deposit insurance, lender of last resort operations conducive to excessive risk taking by banks, and a lack of prudential regulation.

By mid-1982, as problems in the banking system became more prominent, the central bank cast a wide safety net. It began by providing a preferential exchange rate for dollar debtors and buying the banks' bad portfolios at face value. The nonperforming assets of commercial banks were replaced by central bank bonds. The government intervened in the flagship banks of the two largest conglomerates. Furthermore, the government explicitly guaranteed the total outstanding bank debt. In the end, the bailout led to a substantial buildup of central bank debt and quasi-fiscal deficits that continue to be part of today's landscape.[19]

The experience of the 1982–84 banking crisis set the stage for breakthrough reform, in the banking law of 1986. The eventual winners of the new regulation would be the public at large, who had become well aware of the costs of poor regulation. Large conglomerates and owners of commercial banks were poised to lose as the subsidized connected lending would come to an end. In the aftermath of the banking crisis, the new law was designed and adopted in a setting basically void of political constraints of special interests normally binding in reform efforts. The large conglomerates, owners of the largest banks, had been hit hard by the 1982–83 crisis, two prominent bankers were in jail, and all the banks had solvency problems. The banking interest group was thus in a weak position to lobby against new regulations.

Characteristics of Stability-Promoting Banking Institutions

A characteristic of sound banking institutions is that they provide the incentives for depositors and banks to act as if a bailout would be a rare and costly event. An increasingly accepted approach in assessing the vulnerability of a banking system has been to look at regulatory and safety net institutions simultaneously (e.g., Demirgüç-Kunt and

---

[19]For a detailed description of the cost of the bailout, see, for example, Sanhueza (2001).

Kane, 2002; and Boyd and others, 2001). The idea is that bank regulations should be viewed as a complement to market discipline. The degree of market discipline may in turn be affected by the specific type of safety net in place. Depositors' incentives to monitor banks will depend on whether full deposit insurance is anticipated. Similarly, if closure procedures are not clearly defined and enforced, banks may feel they can safely bet on an indiscriminate extension of a safety net in times of trouble (e.g., a highly discretionary role of lender of last resort (LOLR)).

More concretely, suppose the Chilean government stated that there would be no repeat of the early 1980s bailout. Such a commitment would be most likely to prevail:

- If deposit insurance were not too generous;

- If LOLR facilities were used only to face unanticipated short-term liquidity needs of the system;

- If bank regulation were effective in limiting risk taking; and

- If there were timely and public disclosure of relevant prudential and profit indicators of each bank.

The Banking Landscape After 1986

The Superintendency of Banks and Financial Institutions (SBIF) was created in 1925 and is related to the government through the ministry of finance. Over the years, the SBIF has undergone several changes as part of the country's modernization efforts. The SBIF authorizes the creation of new banks and has increasingly gained powers to interpret and enforce regulations.

The banking law of 1986, and subsequent amendments in 1989 and 1997, provided the SBIF with essential new tools to limit risk taking by banks: restriction of business with related parties (Article 84, No. 2); rating the quality of banking investments (Articles 116, 119, and 126); and requiring compliance with Basel capital requirements.

The banking law also fulfilled other essential requirements. It allowed the regulatory body to quickly identify compliance failures to prevent equity holders from rolling over loan losses (Article 15). It stated explicitly and clearly procedures to deal with solvency problems and close banks (Articles 130–39). Furthermore, it protected the property rights of bank creditors and debtors by stating the different capitalization and other workout mechanisms (Articles 118, 120–29, and 140).

Information to Facilitate Private Monitoring and Reduce Moral Hazard

To reduce the moral hazard problem, timely and accurate information should allow depositors to discipline banks and consequently can be an important complement to regulation. When information reveals that banks are engaging in riskier practices, depositors can penalize these banks by withdrawing their deposits. The SBIF requires banks to publish three times a year a detailed report on compliance with capital requirements and has considerably reduced the scope of the banking secrecy laws.

The Safety Net: Deposit Insurance

In principle, deposit insurance reduces incentives for depositors to use the information available to monitor banks. There is still some debate about the net benefits of explicit deposit insurance (see, e.g., Demirgüç-Kunt and Kane, 2002) but there seems to be consensus on the need for the following: an emphasis on the private funding of the explicit deposit insurance; private monitoring to complement official supervision; compulsory membership in the deposit insurance system; and avoiding too-generous deposit insurance.

In Chile, the strategy of the current deposit insurance system has been to state up front less generous deposit insurance rules of the game in order to diminish its negative impact. Prior to the financial crisis of the early 1980s, there had been no explicit deposit insurance in Chile. Yet, in the event of that crisis, the government ended up casting a wide safety net, which included 100 percent deposit insurance. Looking forward, such generous deposit insurance could be problematic, inducing moral hazard and undermining the market discipline that would otherwise limit risk taking. On the other hand, going with no explicit deposit insurance might again end up translating into full implicit insurance. Chile instead moved to an *explicit* but less generous deposit insurance.

In 1986, Chile's new explicit deposit insurance scheme introduced a distinction between sight and time deposits. Since 1986, there has been an explicit 100 percent coverage to sight deposits but term deposits have a cap (for each depositor) of approximately US$2,800.

How "generous" is Chile's deposit insurance? Two recent studies shed some light:

- According to Budnevich and Franken (2003), the current deposit insurance scheme could represent up to 0.7 percent of GDP. This coverage could be classified as relatively less generous when contrasted with other countries' explicit deposit insurance schemes.

- Martinez-Peria and Schmukler (2001) contribute an empirical analysis, using bank-level data for Chile and other countries. They conclude that deposit insurance in Chile is not so generous as to preclude depositors (both small and large) from disciplining banks for risky behavior.

The Safety Net: A Case of Exceptional Liquidity Provision

An unconstrained LOLR role to banks in trouble will exacerbate the central bank–induced moral hazard problem. LOLR facilities should not to used to bail out specific insolvent banks. LOLR should be used to either help *solvent* institutions with adequate collateral meet liquidity shocks with the provision of liquidity at market interest rates or to help the banking system meet unanticipated short-term liquidity needs. An example of a recent deployment of Chile's LOLR facilities is the response of the central bank to the "CORFO-Inverlink" affair (see Section V). This refers to a case of fraud of some significance, involving a financial holding company, that emerged in March 2003. Although this case originated outside the banking system, its repercussions soon extended to the banking system, as it induced many financial market players to seek liquidity urgently.

In response to that shock, during March 10–14, 2003, the central bank provided liquidity through its overnight window, and swap operations in U.S. dollars with resale agreements. As described in Section V, the central bank's liquidity provision did not target a specific bank; instead, it provided liquidity to the system, which subsequently was gradually removed.

Closure Procedures

Are Chilean institutions credible in the sense of providing the right incentives to avoid a repeat of the early 1980s bailout? More specifically, are bank closure procedures clearly defined and credible? Brock (1992) reports two examples illustrating closure procedures at work. In 1988, the Banco del Pacífico was required to increase its loan-loss provisions by 60 percent against bad loans. The funds came from subordinated debt from another bank. In 1989, the SBIF intervened in Banco Nacional after discovering hidden losses. The government did not bail out the banks in either case.

Pending Issues and Questions

We have argued that Chile has achieved a good balance between prudential regulation, market discipline, and not overly generous banking deposit in-surance. However, looking forward, it may be worth reflecting on a few questions.

- Do Chile's banking regulators enjoy adequate legal protection in the exercise of their duties? Legal protection of supervisory staff in the fulfillment of their duties is key to reducing the threat of intimidation. In Chile, the only protection in place is Article 25 of the 1986 banking law but it is specific to the protection of SBIF staff only during a bank intervention.

- Should the structure of the banking system deposit insurance be revised? Consider the following example of how the ever-evolving banking system could affect the central bank's deposit insurance liability. In June 2002, the central bank authorized banks to issue interest-bearing sight deposit accounts. So far, the move has not induced a large switch from noninterest-bearing to interest-bearing accounts—in part due to the low opportunity cost that the current low interest environment represents. However, the situation is likely to change when the central bank switches to a tighter mode. Significant increases in sight deposit accounts would represent a larger potential deposit insurance liability for the central bank. In light of this possibility it might be a good idea to revisit the question of how generous deposit insurance might be.

- Have steps been taken to allow consolidated supervision of the financial system? In response to the CORFO-Inverlink affair, the authorities appended a number of proposals to the capital market reform package that had been already in preparation. Capital Market Reform II (CMII) is an ambitious set of 60 proposals, recently sent to congress, to either modify old or create new laws. CMII includes a proposal to improve *coordination* of the financial system supervisory agencies. It does not include the, in principle, more desirable alternative of consolidation of supervision.

Maintaining an Open Trade Policy Regime: The Role of Institutions

The Problems to Be Confronted

Trade policy is a classic arena for lobbying and rent seeking.[20] The essential problem is that from the point of view of an individual industry, trade protection can bring enormous benefits and so creates in-

---

[20]See Krueger (1974) and Bhagwati and Srinivasan (1980).

centives to lobby for special treatment; on the other hand, the costs of each case of special treatment are usually diffuse, not associated with any particular interest group. One might therefore expect a general tendency toward ever higher and more dispersed rates, yielding high effective rates of protection. Moreover, even if the "common interest" can occasionally break through and generate a reform of the tariff structure, such reform may prove difficult to maintain, if all the factors that previously generated distortions remain in place.

Chile's Trade Policy Experience

In the area of trade policy, Chile has moved from a highly distorted tariff structure to one of the world's most liberal. In the period after World War II, Chile shared with other Latin American countries a strategy of import substitution. Indeed, by the late 1960s, Chile was considered an extreme case, even for the time, in terms of tariff distortion, complexity, and lack of transparency.[21] The military government that took over in 1973 soon implemented a major tariff reform, making Chile the first in the region to break from the import substitution strategy. Subsequently, there was only one significant slippage in the tariff reform, and this turned out to be temporary.[22]

The return to democracy was followed by further trade liberalization. In fact, there have been two further unilateral tariff reductions. In the early 1990s, the uniform external tariff was cut from 15 percent to 11 percent. Starting in the late 1990s, there was a phased reduction of the uniform tariff, from 11 percent to 6 percent (beginning in 1999 and ending in 2003).

How Has a Liberal Trade Regime Been Sustained?

Political economy considerations suggest that a liberal, nondistortionary tariff structure is an economic policy particularly likely to be subject to attack. Chile's success in sustaining such a trade policy has been facilitated by several institutional arrangements:

- *An outright ban on nontariff barriers*, which greatly limits room for industries to lobby for special treatment. This ban has a quasi-constitutional status, being embodied in the Basic Constitutional Act of the Central Bank (amendment of which would require a three-fifths majority of congress).

- *A uniform tariff* also limits the scope for lobbying for special treatment.[23]

- *A transparent tariff-setting process*. Formerly, tariffs were subject to presidential decrees. Foxley and Sapelli (1999) emphasize that the need to discuss tariff changes in congress brought tariff setting "out of the backrooms of bilateral political deals and into the open arena of competitive politics."

Of course, the effect of these institutional arrangements may have been complemented by other factors, such as a deeper appreciation in Chile of the flaws of the import substitution strategy. Certainly, as trade liberalization eventually moved resources into the traded goods sector, it created a growing constituency interested in preserving or deepening liberalization.

Pending Issues in Trade Policy

Chile has been extraordinarily successful in creating and sustaining a liberal trade policy regime. Nevertheless, several second-order issues can be mentioned, in that the uniform external tariff policy does not in fact guarantee a single tariff rate will apply to all imports:

- *"Price bands" scheme for certain agricultural imports*. In place since the 1980s, this system of special, variable import tariffs tends on average to provide some special protection for some agricultural products. However, the list of affected goods is short and has been stable. Moreover, the mechanism for determining these special tariffs is linked to world prices by a nondiscretionary formula, a device that both limits the potential distortion and avoids creating room for lobbying.

- *New trade safeguards law*. This law, enacted several years ago, is consistent with the requirements of the World Trade Organization, but does open a door for individual industries to lobby for special treatment. However, institutional checks should help insulate the process from political pressures. Most importantly, Chile's safeguards law provides for only temporary special protection (expiring automatically after a year, with a maximum renewal of one additional year).

- *Bilateral trade agreements*. During the 1990s, new bilateral trade agreements increased effec-

---

[21]Chile's trade regime may have been among the world's most distorted: tariffs were not only high but also tremendously varied and subject to frequent ad hoc changes.

[22]Prompted by the early 1980s' debt crisis, this temporary deviation was essentially an emergency balance of payments/fiscal revenue measure.

[23]See Panagariya and Rodrik (1993) for a review of political economy arguments for a common tariff.

tive protection for many sectors.[24] The significance of potentially resulting distortions is limited, however, since the level of the uniform tariff is now down to just 6 percent.

Closing Observations

For nearly a generation, the story of Chile's economic development has been mainly a positive one. This section has highlighted some ways in which institutional arrangements have contributed to this success, in particular by fostering the adoption and maintenance of sound policies, in several key areas. While these institutions did not alone determine Chile's course, they are likely to have played an important role.

A further analysis of the Chilean economic experience could look also at how other factors, including other kinds of institutional arrangements, promoted favorable decision making by the public and private sectors, and how certain policies may have been self-reinforcing or helped to build institutions. For example, points along the following lines may have been relevant in the Chilean case:

- Protections on private property, including on foreign investment;

- Openness to foreign capital, in turn generating incentives to move toward international best practices, and to avoid policy errors or unpredictability that might induce capital flight. Similarly, the importance of trade openness may also go beyond the usual gains from trade, serving as an "anchor" for institutional reform; and

- International agreements that may be serving as commitment devices.

Commentators on Chile often emphasize the importance of consensus building in the country's ability to move ahead. While part of the ability to achieve consensus may be due to the political rules discussed earlier, there may be more to the story.

Important work remains for Chile's further economic development, and some of this progress may be associated with institutional enhancements. This section has noted issues pending in several policy areas, but other areas of institutional reform may be possible, such as public sector reform. Indeed, an atypical wave of public corruption and fraud charges that began in late 2002 already has led to major re-

form of the public sector (see IMF, 2003b and 2003c). The prompt response of the Chilean authorities—and of Chilean society—to these unexpected developments has spoken well of the country's institutions, including policymakers' ability to recognize issues and build consensus to confront them. As these reforms begin to be implemented, it will become possible to assess whether further efforts are needed. Also looking ahead, for Chile as for other countries, there will be the ongoing challenge of keeping financial supervision and regulation up with constantly evolving financial markets. An important stocktaking in that regard will begin with the authorities' participation in the IMF's Financial Sector Assessment Program in late 2003.

References

Alesina, A., and L. Summers, 1993, "Central Bank Independence and Macroeconomic Performance: Some Comparative Evidence," *Journal of Money, Credit and Banking,* Vol. 25 (May), pp. 151–62.

Alesina, A., R. Hausmann, R. Hommes, and E. Stein, 1998, "Budget Institutions and Fiscal Performance in Latin America," IADB Working Paper Series No. 394 (Washington: Inter-American Development Bank).

Annett, A., 2002, "Politics, Government Size, and Fiscal Adjustment in Industrial Countries," IMF Working Paper No. 02/162 (Washington: International Monetary Fund).

Barth, J.R., G. Caprio, Jr., and R. Levine, 2002, "Bank Regulation and Supervision: What Works Best?" NBER Working Paper No. 9323 (Cambridge, Massachusetts: National Bureau of Economic Research).

Barro, R.J., and D.B. Gordon, 1983, "A Positive Theory of Monetary Policy in a Natural Rate Model," *Journal of Political Economy*, Vol. 91 (August), pp. 589–610.

Bhagwati, J., and T.N. Srinivasan, 1980, "Revenue Seeking: A Generalization of the Theory of Tariffs," *Journal of Political Economy*, Vol. 88, No. 6 (December), pp. 1069–87.

Boyd, J.H., and A.J. Rolnick, 1988, "A Case for Reforming Federal Deposit Insurance," *Annual Report*, Federal Reserve Bank of Minneapolis.

Boyd, J.H., S. Kwak, and P. Gomis, 2001, " A User's Guide to Banking Crises" (unpublished).

Brock, P., ed., 1992, *If Texas Were Chile: A Primer on Banking Reform* (San Francisco: ICS Press).

Budnevich, C., and H. Franken, 2003, "Disciplina de Mercado en la Conducta de los Depositantes y el Rol de las Agencias Clasificadoras de Riesgo: El Caso de Chile," *Economía Chilena*, Vol. 6, No. 2 (August), pp. 45–70.

Calderón, C., and K. Schmidt-Hebbel, 2003, "Learning the Hard Way: Ten Lessons for Latin America" (unpublished; Santiago: Central Bank of Chile).

Catao, L., and M. Terrones, 2003, "Fiscal Deficits and Inflation," IMF Working Paper No. 03/65 (Washington: International Monetary Fund).

---

[24]Foxley and Sapelli (1999, p. 410) argue that the benefits of Chile's uniform tariff were "in some ways jeopardized by bilateral agreements that increased effective protection for many sectors and abandoned the worthy goal of giving all sectors the same degree of protection."

Central Bank of Chile, 2000, Fourth Annual Conference, "Ten Years of Inflation Targeting: Design, Performance, Challenges," November 30–December 1, Santiago. Available via the Internet at http://www.bcentral.cl/eng/stdpub/conferences/annual/metas2000.htm.

Cochrane, J.H., 2001, "Long Term Debt and Optimal Policy in the Fiscal Theory of the Price Level," *Econometrica*, Vol. 69 (January), pp. 69–116.

Corbo, V., and K. Schmidt-Hebbel, 2001, "Inflation Targeting in Latin America," Central Bank of Chile Working Paper No. 105 (Santiago: Central Bank of Chile).

Cukierman, A., 1992, *Central Bank Strategy, Credibility, and Independence: Theory and Evidence* (Cambridge, Massachusetts: MIT Press).

Danninger, S., 2002, "The Swiss Debt Brake," IMF Working Paper No. 02/18 (Washington: International Monetary Fund).

Davis, J., R. Ossowski, J. Daniel, and S. Barnett, 2001, "Stabilization and Savings Funds for Nonrenewable Resources: Experience and Fiscal Policy Implications," IMF Occasional Paper No. 205 (Washington: International Monetary Fund).

De Gregorio, J., 2003, "Mucho Dinero y Poca Inflación: Chile y la Evidencia Internacional," Central Bank of Chile, Economic Policy Papers, Vol. 8 (September).

de la Cuadra, S., and S. Valdes, 1992, "Myths and Facts About Financial Liberalization in Chile: 1974–83," in *If Texas Were Chile: A Primer on Banking Reform*, ed. by P. Brock (San Francisco: ICS Press).

Demirgüç-Kunt, A., and E.J. Kane, 2002, "Deposit Insurance: Handle with Care," paper presented at the Sixth Annual Conference of the Central Bank of Chile on Banking Industry and Monetary Policy, November, Santiago.

Foxley, A., 2003, "Development Lessons of the 1990s: Chile," paper presented at the World Bank Conference Series "Practitioners of Development," Washington.

Foxley, A., and C. Sapelli, 1999, "Chile's Political Economy in the 1990s: Some Governance Issues," in *Chile: Recent Policy Lessons and Emerging Challenges*, ed. by G. Perry and D. Leipziger (Washington: World Bank).

Gutiérrez, E., 2003, "Inflation Performance and Constitutional Central Bank Independence: Evidence from Latin America and the Caribbean," IMF Working Paper No. 03/53 (Washington: International Monetary Fund).

International Monetary Fund, 2003a, "Growth and Institutions," Chapter III in *World Economic Outlook, April*, World Economic and Financial Surveys (Washington).

———, 2003b, "Chile: 2003 Article IV Consultation—Staff Report; Staff Statement; Public Information Notice on the Executive Board Discussion; and Statement by the Executive Director for Chile," IMF Country Report No. 03/303 (Washington: International Monetary Fund).

———, 2003c, "Chile: Report on the Observance of Standards and Codes—Fiscal Transparency Module," IMF Country Report No. 03/237 (Washington: International Monetary Fund).

Jones, M.P., P. Sanguinetti, and M. Tommaso, 2000, "Politics, Institutions, and Fiscal Performance in a Federal System: An Analysis of the Argentine Provinces," *Journal of Development Economics*, Vol. 61 (April), pp. 305–33.

Kydland, F., and E. Prescott, 1977, "Rules Rather Than Discretion: The Inconsistency of Optimal Plans," *Journal of Political Economy*, Vol. 85 (June), pp. 473–91.

Krueger, A.O., 1974, "The Political Economy of the Rent-Seeking Society," *American Economic Review*, Vol. 64, No. 3 (June), pp. 291–303.

Laval Z., J. Esteban, and J. Carrasco Vásquez, 2000, "Banco Central de Chile: Preceptos Constitucionales Ley Orgánica y Legislación Complementaria" (August).

Labán, R., and F. Larraín, 1998, "The Return of Private Capital to Chile in the 1990s: Causes, Effects and Policy Reactions," Development Discussion Paper No. 627 (Cambridge, Massachusetts: Harvard Institute for International Development).

Martinez Peria, M.S., and S.L. Schmukler, 2001, "Do Depositors Punish Banks for Bad Behavior? Market Discipline, Deposit Insurance, and Banking Crises," *Journal of Finance*, Vol. 56, No. 3 (June), pp. 1029–51.

Morandé, F., 2001, "A Decade of Inflation Targeting in Chile: Developments, Lessons and Challenges," Central Bank of Chile Working Paper No. 115 (Santiago: Central Bank of Chile).

———, and M. Tapia, 2002, "Exchange Rate Policy in Chile: From the Band to Floating and Beyond," Central Bank of Chile Working Paper No. 152 (Santiago: Central Bank of Chile).

Orphanides A. and J. Williams, 2002, "Imperfect Knowledge, Inflation Expectations and Monetary Policy," Economic Research Department Working Paper No. 2002/04 (San Francisco: Federal Reserve Bank of San Francisco).

Panagariya, A., and D. Rodrick, 1993, "Political-Economy Arguments for a Uniform Tariff," *International Economic Review*, Vol. 34, No. 3 (August), pp. 685–703.

Sargent, T., and N. Wallace, 1982, "Some Unpleasant Monetarist Arithmetic," *Federal Reserve Bank of Minneapolis Quarterly Review*, Vol. 9, No. 1 (Winter), pp. 15–31.

Sanhueza, G., 2001, "Chilean Banking Crisis of the 1980s: Solutions and Estimation of the Costs," Central Bank of Chile Working Paper No. 104 (Santiago: Central Bank of Chile).

Schmidt-Hebbel, K., and M. Tapia, 2002, "Monetary Policy Implementation and Results in Twenty Inflation-Targeting Countries," Central Bank of Chile Working Paper No.166 (Santiago: Central Bank of Chile).

Sims, C., 2003, "Limits to Inflation Targeting." Available via the Internet at www.sims.princeton.edu/yftp/Targeting/TargetingFiscalPaper.pdf.

Stein, E., E. Talvi and A. Grisanti, 1999, "Institutional Arrangements and Fiscal Performance: The Latin American Experience," in *Fiscal Institutions and Fiscal Performance*, ed. by J.M. Poterba and J. von Hagen (Chicago: University of Chicago Press).

Woodford, M., 2001, "Fiscal Requirements for Price Stability," *Journal of Money, Credit and Banking*, Vol. 33 (August), pp. 69–116.

III   Chile's Macroeconomic Policy Framework

Steven Phillips and Marco A. Espinosa-Vega

Chile's macroeconomic policy framework[1]—with central bank policies focused on inflation targeting, in the context of a floating exchange rate, and fiscal policy following a structural balance target—is still relatively recent (see Box 3.1 for a sypnopsis). This section documents the essential points of this framework's design, highlighting aspects that may distinguish it from other countries' related practices as well as some recent refinements. Also discussed are the track record to date and various implementation issues that have turned out to be relevant in the last few years.

Inflation targeting in Chile had its beginnings around 1990. Price stability is one of the primary mandates in the central bank's 1989 charter.[2] From 1989 to 2000, the bank used one-year-ahead forecasts of end-year inflation to help anchor expectations, treating these forecasts essentially as short-run targets. During those years, the emphasis was on gradual disinflation, and a new, lower short-run inflation target was announced each year. The announced longer-run objective was convergence of inflation to a level similar to that of industrial countries. Indeed, inflation declined gradually, from close to 30 percent in 1990 to less than 3 percent in 1999, though it continued to exhibit some volatility.

Full-fledged inflation targeting emerged more recently. In September 1999, the central bank announced its intention to adopt, at the beginning of 2001, what is now known as the inflation-targeting framework. The essential elements of this framework in Chile include (1) a prespecified continuous inflation target band; (2) a preannounced "policy horizon"; and (3) timely communication of the central bank's inflation forecast, the rationale for its monetary policy decisions, and the reasons for any temporary deviations from the inflation target.

In this framework, the objective of monetary policy is to maintain inflation at a continuous target at the midpoint of the 2–4 percent target band,[3] by looking ahead to inflation over the policy horizon of one to two years (a widely accepted lag for the effects of monetary policy). The targeted variable is the easily verifiable consumer price index ("headline") inflation rate. The monetary policy stance is evaluated, and adjusted as necessary, at least once a month, in light of the central bank's updated inflation forecast.

The bank's operating target, or policy instrument, is the (nominal) overnight interest rate. In August 2001, the bank switched to a nominal interest rate target, ending its long-standing practice of targeting the interest rate on the Unidad de Fomento, Chile's inflation-indexed unit of account. Since then, the bank has been in the process of "nominalizing" its balance sheet as well, reducing its inflation-indexed liabilities, and extending the maturity range of its unindexed liabilities.

The central bank regularly forecasts both headline and core inflation; these forecasts are the basis for monetary policy actions.[4] The bank's inflation forecast relies on econometric models and judgment based on the output gap, the unemployment rate, the outlook for the world economy, commodity prices, and the stance of fiscal policy, the exchange rate, and firms' markups. Monetary aggregates have little weight in the forecasting models, since the bank has found these to have little predictive value for inflation (once other variables are accounted for).[5]

---

[1]This section focuses on monetary, exchange rate, and fiscal policies. The Chilean authorities have emphasized that these policies are part of a broader policy framework, which also includes international financial integration with an open capital account, modern financial regulation and supervision, and prudent management of liquidity in foreign currency.

[2]The central bank has been nominally independent since the passage of the 1980 constitution. The enactment of the central bank's organic law in 1989 granted full independence to the bank.

[3]Interestingly, by continuously guarding against persistent deviations from either bound, symmetric inflation targets such as Chile's have become an essential tool against deflation.

[4]The core measure excludes fuel and some food items.

[5]A recent bank study shows that in Chile M1A growth has had little predictive power over the inflation rate during the 1986–2002 period, and that the predictive value of M1A is greatly diminished when additional explanatory variables, such as external inflation, are added to the forecasting model. A recent survey paper from the bank (see De Gregorio, 2003) also finds that in low-inflation economies where monetary policy enjoys credibility, periods of higher money supply growth have not resulted in higher inflation.

Box 3.1. Steps in the Development of Chile's Macroeconomic Policy Framework

September 1999	Central bank announces:
	• Continuous inflation target, to start in 2001.
	• Elimination of exchange rate band in favor of floating rate (retaining right to intervene in exceptional circumstances only).
March 2000	New government commits itself to a fiscal policy target: structural surplus of 1 percent of GDP to be maintained throughout the government's six-year term.
May 2000	Central bank issues first Monetary Policy Report—to be published regularly, every four months.
September 2000	Government publishes rationale and methodology for fiscal target. 2001 budget submission formulated to achieve fiscal target.
July 2001	Central bank declares exceptional circumstances and announces first instance of exchange market intervention under floating regime, specifying limits on duration and magnitude of intervention.
August 2001	Expert panel convened for first time to determine reference price of copper to be used in structural balance measure.
August 2002	Expert panel convened for first time to provide inputs to fiscal target's potential output estimate.
October 2002	New debt report clarifies public sector balance sheet and solvency.

The central bank's inflation forecast and its view of risks have been clearly articulated through a number of outlets, including the policy statements of the bank's board, minutes of the regular monthly policy meetings, and a sophisticated Monetary Policy Report issued three times a year. In addition, the bank has made public an overview of its forecasting models and intends to start publishing these on a regular basis.

Significantly, Chile's inflation target is not revised in response to unforeseen inflation developments; indeed, the target has remained unchanged since the adoption of the framework.

The track record under inflation targeting has been favorable:

• Actual inflation has generally remained inside the target band (Figure 3.1). Both headline and core inflation rates, measured on a 12-month basis, have generally remained between 2 percent and 4 percent. Stays near the upper and lower boundaries have occurred, in association with temporary sharp movements in key relative prices. The two visits to the top of the band were linked to sharp increases in oil import prices. The visit to the bottom of the band has been associated with a period of "imported deflation."

• Indicators of inflation expectations have also been consistent with the inflation target (Figure 3.2). In the bank's monthly survey of 12-month-ahead inflation forecasts, the median forecast has been very close to 3 percent. Other expectations indicators, the differentials between interest rates on inflation-indexed and nominal debt at horizons of one to five years, also have stayed close to 3 percent.

The Floating Exchange Rate Regime

In September 1999, the central bank announced that it was discontinuing its long-standing exchange rate band, in favor of a floating exchange rate. More precisely, the bank stated its intention to forsake any intervention in the foreign exchange market under normal circumstances. Henceforth, intervention would occur only after the bank had identified exceptional circumstances, in which case the authorities would explain their rationale for intervening and publish data revealing the amount of intervention.

The authorities have clarified their concept of such exceptional circumstances. They consider that exceptional circumstances are situations in which a sudden shift in market participants' confidence, un-

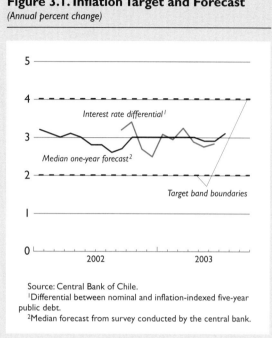

Figure 3.1. Inflation Target and Forecast
(Annual percent change)

Source: Central Bank of Chile.
[1]Differential between nominal and inflation-indexed five-year public debt.
[2]Median forecast from survey conducted by the central bank.

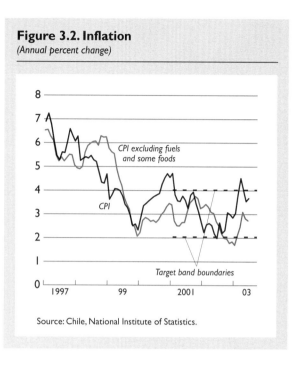

Figure 3.2. Inflation
(Annual percent change)

Source: Chile, National Institute of Statistics.

related to long-term fundamentals, could result in sharp transitory shifts in the value of the peso, a steep reduction of the dollar value of peso-denominated Chilean assets leading to a loss of confidence, and expectations of further depreciation of the exchange rate. Such developments could potentially have significant negative real effects or result in a loss of control over monetary policy and interest rates.[6]

Since the free float was announced, the central bank has identified and declared two periods of exceptional circumstances: one beginning in July 2001 and the other in October 2002. In both instances, the peso had recently experienced significant depreciation pressures in the face of regional uncertainties (in 2001, related mainly to Argentina, and in 2002 to Brazil). In an effort to preempt excessive volatility without targeting a specific exchange rate, both interventions consisted of announcing predetermined caps on the sale of official reserves in the spot market and on net issuance of (medium-term) dollar-indexed bonds, over an announced period.

- During the first such intervention period, the authorities decided to step up issuance of paper indexed to the exchange rate for a period of up to

six months, beginning July 2001. The sales cap on these instruments was set at US$3.5 billion, while the cap on the spot market intervention was set at US$2 billion. In the event, during the second half of 2001, the bank sold reserves of only about US$0.8 billion in the spot market, while it carried out net issuance of dollar-indexed bonds worth US$2.3 billion.

- In the second intervention episode, a similar "package" was again announced at the outset. This included identical caps of US$2 billion for the net issuance of dollar-indexed bonds and spot intervention for a maximum period of four months—from early October 2002 to early February 2003. In the event, the bank sold no reserves in the spot market but did raise the stock of its dollar-indexed debt by about US$1½ billion.

Thus intervention has consisted mainly of issuance of (medium-term) dollar-indexed debt. The authorities have explained that their preference to intervene in the exchange rate market via dollar debt issuance aims fundamentally at preserving the bank's liquidity position in foreign currency. Accordingly, the bank has avoided any short-term issues of such debt; maturities have ranged from two to five years.

The exchange rate interventions and the authorities' exchange rate management in general have been transparent. On the days when the bank intervened in the spot market, it announced that this had occurred.

---

[6]See also the explanation of intervention published in the bank's January 2003 Monetary Policy Report: http://www.bcentral.cl/esp/estpub/publicaciones/politicas/polit02.htm.

Every two weeks,[7] the bank has released not only its net international reserve position, but also a table decomposing its recent changes into several sources, of which one represents spot market intervention. As for intervention via issuance of dollar-indexed debt, the amount of such debt is published once a month as part of the IMF's standard template on reserves and foreign currency liquidity; the total is also published on a daily basis on the bank's web site.[8]

During both intervention episodes, the bank made clear that it had no target for the exchange rate. The pattern of intervention bears out this claim. The issuance of dollar-indexed debt did not respond to day-to-day exchange rate fluctuations; rather, it followed a preannounced schedule over the intervention period and within each month. As for spot market intervention, the days on which this occurred do not correspond to times of the greatest weakness of the peso.[9]

Fiscal Policy: Targeting the Government's Structural Balance

Soon after taking office in March 2000, Chile's new government committed itself to an ongoing target for the structural balance of the central government.[10] The government announced that it would measure its structural balance essentially by making two cyclical adjustments to its actual balance: one for the effect of the output gap, and the other for the effect of variations in copper export prices.[11]

In announcing that it would seek to hold this structural balance at a constant level over its six-year term, the government defined a medium-term fiscal policy path, or rule:

- The government thus gave up future discretion over the underlying fiscal stance. Henceforth, the level of government expenditure would be tied to the level of structural (i.e., cyclically adjusted) revenue. At the margin, any policy proposal that would change government expendi-

ture or revenue would have to be associated with a plan for other, offsetting policy measures.

- By targeting the structural rather than actual balance, the government was able to commit itself to a precise target without having to suppress automatic stabilizers.

- In principle, holding the structural balance steady means a policy of full and immediate policy adjustment to permanent shocks, with zero policy adjustment to temporary shocks.

Although Chile's fiscal policy is sometimes said to be "countercyclical," this term is subject to misunderstanding; it may be better to say that the rule avoids procyclical policies and allows operation of automatic stabilizers. More precisely:

- The rule does not permit government expenditure to move at all countercyclically; for example, there is no room to temporarily raise government expenditure during an economic downturn. Nor is there room to cut tax rates.

- At the same time, the policy also does not permit procyclical policy reactions (i.e., expenditure would not be cut back with a view to compensating for lower tax collection in a recession).

The essence of the rule is thus the nonresponse of government expenditure (or tax rates) to temporary fluctuations in output and copper prices. What instead moves in synchronization with these cycles is the actual government *balance*. While fluctuation may be called countercyclical, the authorities have not emphasized the possible Keynesian-type effects of this policy in dampening recessions or tempering overheating.

Rather than a means to stabilize output, the authorities have emphasized several other objectives of their structural balance target. These include avoiding inefficiencies of erratic shifts in government expenditure, maintaining the solvency of the state, signaling medium-term policy intentions, and enhancing transparency and accountability of fiscal policy. They have also emphasized the consistency of this fiscal policy with the monetary and exchange rate policies of the central bank. In particular, fiscal discipline allows monetary policy to operate more effectively, and in the absence of an exchange rate target, monetary policy recently has been able to play an active countercyclical role (in the context of inflation targeting).

The policy of aiming at a specific, "point" target in every year is demanding—in particular, compared with practices elsewhere calling for balance over the business cycle or the medium term. Relatedly, the structural balance rule is also technically demanding, requiring that fluctuations in output (and copper prices) be identified, as they occur in real time, as ei-

---

[7]Since mid-2003, reserves data are now published weekly.

[8]See http://www.bcentral.cl/esp/estpub/publicaciones/financiera ycambiaria/finacam01.htm.

[9]Notably, within the preannounced intervention periods, the bank refrained from intervening, as the peso slid in the days after September 11, 2001; in late October 2001, when the peso reached its weakest point for that year; and in early February 2003, as the peso approached a new record low.

[10]More detailed discussions of the rationale and methodology of the structural balance target can be found in Ministry of Finance (2001) and IMF (2001), Chapter II. Refinements made since those papers were prepared are discussed in this section.

[11]The government is sole owner of a copper company, CODELCO.

ther temporary or permanent. Implementation of the rule has to be based on necessarily uncertain estimates. The approach is therefore heavy on technique and centered on concepts that are abstract and unobservable (i.e., potential output and the underlying price of copper). In such a context, transparency and communication are likely to be especially important, and indeed the authorities have stepped up their efforts on these fronts since the rule was adopted.

Specific Aspects of the Chilean Fiscal Policy Framework

Before examining implications of these issues, and the Chilean approaches to dealing with them, it is useful to review some of the essential attributes of the Chilean fiscal policy framework:

- *No legal basis.* Among policy rules, Chile's framework is relatively informal. The target is a self-imposed commitment of the current government, without a legal basis of its own or any type of formal mechanism to enforce compliance. Instead, the legal basis for the fiscal stance in each year is the annual budget law, which does limit government expenditure; it is the government's policy to submit to congress each year a budget designed to be consistent with the structural balance target. Because the budget process rules in Chile largely favor the executive over the legislature, the latter is unlikely to be able to alter decisions made by the former in compliance with the structural balance rule.

- *A point target applies to each budget year.* There is no target band to allow year-to-year discretion (nor to suggest what is an acceptable or normal degree of deviation from the target). If the fiscal outturn deviates from the target, the policy target for the following year is not affected; that is, there is no commitment to offset past deviations.

- *The chosen target level is an annual surplus of 1 percent of GDP for the central government accounts.* The government has explained the need for a surplus in terms of several considerations: offsetting the quasi-fiscal losses of the central bank; as a precaution against several potentially important contingent liabilities; and to at least partly offset the effect on net worth of selling the state's copper resources.

- *Cyclical adjustment is relatively small, for a given output gap.* No allowance for cyclical effects is made on the expenditure side. The adjustment on the revenue side is limited by the approximately 20 percent share of government revenue in GDP (thus, as a rule of thumb, each

1 percent deviation of actual from potential output implies an estimated cyclical revenue effect of 0.2 percent of GDP).[12]

- *The total cyclical adjustment includes also a component related to copper price fluctuations.* In 2001 and 2002, years of relatively low copper prices, this adjustment was about 1 percent of GDP.[13]

- *The target applies to the entire government balance—including interest payments and capital expenditure.* Notably, a hypothetical increase in market interest rates faced by the government would require policy measures to raise the primary balance enough to offset the higher interest bill.

- *The structural balance is not derived directly from the official budget and statistical definition of the government balance.* Before cyclical adjustments are applied, the traditional government balance is adjusted in several ways to better capture changes in the government's net worth. However, the authorities are in the process of revamping the official statistics, following the new standard set out in the IMF's *Government Finance Statistics Manual 2001*, with a view to unification of their fiscal presentations.

The Chilean approach probably has its closest international parallel in Switzerland's fiscal framework, in that a specific point target level is established for each year, with a cyclical adjustment made on the revenue side only. As in Chile, the Swiss rule constrains all spending by the central government, not just its current expenditures. However, the Swiss approach differs in several ways, including in being constitutionally based and therefore more permanent in nature, in defining escape clauses from the rule, and in requiring that a shortfall from the target in one year be offset in subsequent years.[14]

Some Implementation Issues

In implementing the target, there is the practical challenge of distinguishing temporary from perma-

---

[12]In member countries of the Organization for Economic Cooperation and Development, for which estimates of structural budget balances are more familiar than in developing countries, estimates of cyclical effects are usually considerably higher, both because of the larger share of taxes in GDP and because adjustments are also made on the expenditure side.

[13]IMF (2002), Chapter III, examines the long-run properties of copper prices, with a particular application to the Chilean fiscal policy context.

[14]Strictly speaking, the Swiss approach also differs in that it involves an expenditure, rather than a deficit, target. However, the expenditure target is tied to cyclically adjusted revenue. See Danninger (2002) for a full analysis of the Swiss approach.

nent shocks as they occur in real time. Since cyclical effects cannot be observed, even ex post, they must be estimated. Contemporaneous estimates of output gaps are known to be especially subject to revision.[15]

Beginning with the 2002 budget, the Chilean authorities refined their fiscal policy framework by delegating to an expert panel the determination of copper price gap; starting with the 2003 budget, expert input was also used to estimate the output gap.

- A few months before each annual budget is prepared, a committee is convened to directly provide the copper "reference price." Minutes of this meeting are published, including each member's individual forecast. Each member is required to provide a forecast of the average copper price over the coming 10 years (rather than a notional long-run price or equilibrium price). The reference price is then determined as the average of these forecasts, after excluding highest and lowest values.

- To estimate potential output, an expert committee is also convened, though it does not directly provide an estimate of potential output. Rather, each member provides medium-term forecasts of the critical input variables (productivity, capital stock, and so on) for the authorities' algorithm for estimating potential output. This algorithm is based on a published methodology, and combines an estimated production function with the use of the Hodrick-Prescott filter to smooth the data. Within this framework, the committee also engages the authorities in methodological discussions. Minutes of this committee's meetings are made public.

This use of expert committees in measuring the structural balance is a significant step in assuring the transparency and credibility of the fiscal policy rule. While this procedure cannot eliminate uncertainty over the accuracy of the structural balance measure, perfect accuracy is not essential to the objectives of the policy.

In the last few years, a variety of shocks have made achieving the structural balance target in a given year more complicated than simply setting expenditure to increase in line with growth of potential output:

- *Structural revenue is not constant as a share of GDP.* On the positive side, the government occasionally benefits from one-time revenue windfalls; in some cases, the government has dealt with these by excluding such revenue from the measured structural balance. Another positive factor for the government has been the real exchange rate depreciation of the last few years, which raised (cyclically adjusted) copper receipts as a share of GDP.

- *Inflation surprises, in either direction.* For example, in 2002, lower-than-expected inflation led to a revenue shortfall.

- *Revisions to previous estimates of the level of potential output.* In preparing the 2003 budget, the government avoided this problem by adhering to its previous estimate of 2002 potential output as a base, applying to that figure the growth rate of potential output determined by the expert panel.

Relatedly, in two of the first three years of implementation of the structural balance rule the government announced around midyear that it would hold expenditure below budgeted levels in order to achieve the structural balance target.

Market Reaction and Public Ownership

Market confidence in the soundness of Chilean fiscal policy—as indicated by international bond spreads and credit ratings—has continued to be high. This confidence likely has been supported in part by the self-imposed constraint of the new structural balance rule, though also by a more general faith in Chilean institutions and political consensus in favor of fiscal policy discipline.

Outside of Chile, awareness and understanding of the structural balance target have gradually increased. As many other emerging market economies had to run procyclical fiscal policies during the recent downturn in the world economy, many commentators noted—generally with favor—that Chile was allowing automatic stabilizers to operate, in the controlled manner dictated by the structural balance rule. After the 2003 budget was submitted, a few analysts did issue critical reports, arguing that the levels of Chile's fiscal balance and fiscal data transparency did not justify the country's strong credit rating and low bond spreads. Although the criticism of the fiscal stance was soon rebutted by other analysts, the authorities stepped up their efforts to explain the structural balance rule, issued a new report on the debt and liquid public assets of the entire public sector, and began an enhanced schedule of fiscal data releases.

---

[15]Gallego and Johnson (2003) show confidence intervals for output gap estimates constructed with the Hodrick-Prescott filter. Looking at the G-7 countries, they find that confidence intervals are fairly wide in general and tend to flare out at the end of the sample.

The extent of ownership of the structural balance target is as yet difficult to judge. The government's commitment to its own structural balance target appears very strong, indeed as one of the flagship policies of the administration of President Lagos. Given the budget process rules in Chile, this ingredient alone practically assures the implementation of the rule over the final three years of the government's term. Outside the current administration, there seems to be a broad political consensus in favor of the principle of maintaining fiscal discipline; however, it is as yet unclear whether the particular mechanisms of the structural balance rule would be endorsed, in whole or in part, by future administrations. In terms of current political debate, it seems that the structural balance rule has shifted the focus away from the underlying fiscal stance (widely perceived to have deteriorated excessively in the late 1990s before recovering in 2000–01) and toward questions of the appropriate size of government.

References

Danninger, S., 2002, "A New Rule: 'The Swiss Debt Brake,'" IMF Working Paper No. 02/18 (Washington: International Monetary Fund).

De Gregorio, J., 2003, "Mucho Dinero y Poca Inflación: Chile y La Evidencia Internacional," Central Bank of Chile, Economic Policy Papers, Vol. 8 (Santiago).

Gallego, F.A., and C.A. Johnson, 2003, "Building Confidence Intervals for the Band-Pass and Hodrick-Prescott Filters: An Application Using Bootstrapping," Central Bank of Chile Working Paper No. 202 (Santiago: Central Bank of Chile).

International Monetary Fund, 2001, *Chile: Selected Issues*, IMF Country Report No. 01/120 (Washington: International Monetary Fund).

———, 2002, *Chile: Selected Issues*, IMF Country Report No. 02/163 (Washington: International Monetary Fund).

Ministry of Finance, 2001, "Structural Budget Balance," available via the Internet at http://www.dipres.cl/english/docs/structural_balance.html.

IV Capital Markets and Corporate Financing: Recent Developments

Rodolfo Luzio

The development of local securities markets is an important factor driving financial market development and contributing to economic growth. During the 1990s, Chile experienced a remarkable expansion of domestic capital markets. Rapid financial integration, capital accumulation, and economic growth harnessed a virtuous cycle leading to increasing financial deepening.[1] Following the Asian crisis, the pace of financial deepening in Chile slowed. This change was linked to a number of interrelated developments, including a deterioration of the external environment, a substantial slowdown of real domestic growth, and a downward shift in domestic demand, especially for investment expenditure.[2] Net capital inflows from abroad were much reduced after 1998, a shift that appears to reflect lower demand at least as much as reduced supply of capital.[3] Since 2000, a sharp drop in domestic interest rates has led to a pickup in domestic corporate bond issuance.

The recent resurgence of domestic bond financing has underscored the role of domestic capital markets as providing alternative and flexible sources of financing for the corporate sector. Given the prevailing low domestic interest rate environment, domestic corporate firms have taken advantage of a burgeoning domestic bond market to reduce their foreign exposure and reliance on bank financing. Institutional investors, led by pension funds, have also increased their demand for fixed-income paper following the lackluster return from equities in recent years.

This section reviews the development of domestic capital markets and corporate sector financing in Chile in recent years. The purpose is to describe the main factors contributing to financial deepening and to draw on the policy challenges to promote domestic capital markets as stable sources of funding for the corporate sector. In doing so, the section addresses the following set of questions:

- What have been the main factors underpinning the growth of domestic capital markets in the 1990s?

- What are the main sources and features of Chilean corporate financing?

- What are the main characteristics of the investor base and the role of institutional investors?

- What are the main challenges to promote deeper and more liquid domestic capital markets?

The section underscores the role of macroeconomic policies and structural reforms as the driving factors underpinning the development of local securities markets in the 1990s. Sound monetary and fiscal policies allowed a favorable investment environment, while structural reforms involving privatization and tax policy provided the appropriate conditions for the development of the equity market. Finally, financial sector reforms through early pension fund reform and banking sector regulation assured the sustainability and continuous growth of financial intermediation and sources of funds for firms.

While equity markets saw a rapid expansion in the early 1990s, domestic bank lending remained the leading source of (outside) funding for the corporate sector. The section presents some evidence that firms attempt to "time the market" with their financing sources. Large corporate firms sought to shift from external to domestic financing in the late 1990s, and then progressively moved away from domestic short-term bank borrowing toward long-term bond financing since 2000.[4] The sharp drop in domestic

---

[1]See Eyzaguirre and Lefort (1999) for an overview of these developments.

[2]See Caballero (2002) for an account of the impact of external shocks on domestic output and the effect of lower external savings on domestic investment. In particular, he notes the financial squeeze on small and medium-sized enterprises.

[3]Only for 1998 is it clear that Chilean firms faced restricted access to debt financing, as evidenced by a jump in secondary market bond spreads. Subsequently, such evidence shows that Chilean firms—or at least the large companies that have borrowed externally in the past—have enjoyed ready access to external finance on favorable terms.

[4]Caballero (2002) also provides evidence on the shift of large corporate firms toward domestic bank financing at the expense of small and medium-sized companies. He underscores the perverse economic implications of the crowding-out effect on such companies, which were severely constrained on the financial side.

interest rates helped reduce the costs of issuing long-term bonds in local currency, thus favoring long-duration debt issuance over short-term bank borrowing. Similarly, given the increase in book-to-market ratios of capital since the late 1990s, equity issuance collapsed in favor of debt financing.

The presence of a well-developed and large institutional investor base has played a fundamental role in supporting the demand for domestic paper. The large presence of pension and insurance companies has provided a stable and growing source of investment funds for the corporate sector. These investors have allowed increased specialization in the investment decision-making process and promoted a sophisticated risk-rating industry. They have also encouraged the development of long-term instruments and contributed to improved corporate governance, transparency, and financial sophistication.

Nonetheless, low liquidity and a high degree of ownership and investor concentration remain important challenges for the development of domestic capital markets. While low liquidity in the equity market provides a disincentive to investor participation, it is also related to the high degree of ownership concentration. The prevalence of dominant economic groups continues to characterize the corporate ownership structure and helps explain the financing structure of corporations. The large presence of these groups has raised questions about the shallowness of equity markets, the protection of minority shareholder rights, and the effectiveness of corporate governance. Recent changes in financial sector regulation and legislation have sought to strengthen corporate governance, improve transparency, and guarantee minority shareholder rights. Changes in capital market legislation have also included tax incentives to promote liquidity in equity markets and have sought to increase firms' access to capital markets by reducing issuance costs.

Similarly, investor participation has remained concentrated on institutional investors dominated by pension funds and insurance companies. While the presence of these investors has had several positive effects, they have not contributed to higher market liquidity. These investors have favored buy-and-hold investment strategies and skewed the demand for high-quality paper. Recent changes in financial regulation have sought, however, to ease investment restrictions for institutional investors and promote more flexibility in their investment strategies.

This section is organized as follows. First, it provides an overview of the development of capital markets in the 1990s, noting the factors that contributed to financial deepening. It then describes the corporate sector's increasing reliance on domestic capital markets in the post–Asian crisis period and seeks to explain how firms attempt to "time the market" with

their financing sources. Next, it describes the role of institutional investors as key sources of stability and growth. Then the main challenges for the development of local securities are discussed, including recent financial policy reform initiatives to promote financial deepening. The last section concludes.

Domestic Capital Market Development and Foreign Financing

The domestic capital market in Chile underwent a dramatic transformation in the 1990s, marked by large external capital inflows. In fact, since the late 1980s, Chile has experienced a remarkable process of financial deepening. By end-2002, the ratio of total financial assets to GDP was 225 percent, more than three times the ratio prevailing in 1985. By 2002, the stock market capitalization was still the largest single financial market asset, amounting to 75 percent of GDP, while the bank lending portfolio accounted for 70 percent of GDP. Also significant, central bank bonds, which account for three-quarters of total public sector liabilities, represented 30 percent of GDP, while nonfinancial private sector bonds topped 10 percent by end-2002 (Table 4.1).

From an international perspective, Chile's financial asset accumulation is also remarkable. After controlling for per capita income and output growth, Chile shows a high degree of financial deepening. The results from regressions of the average market capitalization-to-GDP and total asset-to-GDP ratios during the 1990s on per capita income in 1997 and the average growth of per capita income for a sample of 48 countries places Chile significantly above the expected averages (Figure 4.1).[5]

International financial integration represented one of the key catalysts driving the rapid deepening of domestic markets. Asset accumulation accelerated rapidly in the 1990s, while capital flows poured in before experiencing a slowdown at the end of the decade. During the 1990s, foreign direct investment represented the main source of foreign capital flows. By 2002, Chile's liabilities from foreign direct investment had reached 68 percent of GDP, representing about 54 percent of all gross foreign liabilities. Foreign bank loans also became a major source of financing for the private sector. The stock of foreign loans amounted to 41 percent of GDP, accounting for one-third of all gross foreign liabilities (Figure 4.2).

Compared with other emerging market countries, Chile's international investment position underscores the openness of the capital account and the

---

[5]See Demirgüç-Kunt and Levine (2001) for the data source.

Table 4.1. Financial Assets—Outstanding Stocks
(In percent of GDP)

	Corporate Sector			Financial Sector		Public Sector		
	Stock market capitalization	Outstanding bonds	Bank credit	Mortgage bonds	Time deposits	Central bank paper	Central government	Public enterprises
1990	44.9		70.7	5.0	16.9	34.4	20.5	7.6
1991	78.2		59.5	5.0	17.9	31.4	16.9	4.2
1992	66.4		57.3	5.7	19.1	31.0	13.6	3.3
1993	111.5		62.6	6.5	20.3	29.8	11.9	2.6
1994	115.7		51.9	7.6	20.2	30.4	9.6	2.3
1995	101.4	3.4	51.0	8.7	22.0	28.5	6.0	2.2
1996	89.6	3.1	54.4	10.2	25.5	30.0	4.5	2.4
1997	91.0	2.4	57.2	11.8	28.3	31.5	3.4	2.9
1998	67.2	2.9	61.3	11.7	32.0	28.6	3.4	4.2
1999	97.0	3.7	69.2	13.1	34.3	30.3	4.2	4.3
2000	84.7	5.2	69.5	12.9	34.6	31.3	3.9	4.4
2001	85.3	9.3	69.8	13.0	33.6	31.1	4.8	4.9
2002	75.6	11.6	69.2	12.5	34.3	30.5	6.1	6.2

Sources: Central Bank of Chile; Bloomberg; Superintendency of Securities and Insurance; and Superintendency of Pension Fund Administrators.

Figure 4.1. Level of Financial Development for a Sample of Countries

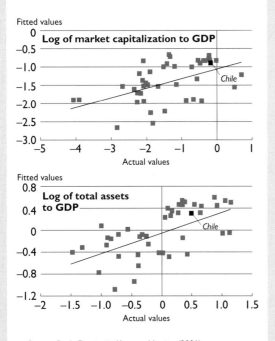

Source: Beck, Demirgüç-Kunt, and Levine (2001).
Note: Fitted values result from regression on average per capita GDP growth from 1990 to 1997 and log of per capita income for 1997.

degree of financial integration. By end-2001, Chile's total foreign liabilities had reached 122 percent of GDP, the highest level among the selected group of countries shown in Figure 4.3. Nonetheless, the stock of foreign direct investment in Chile was also the largest as a ratio to GDP, and represented more than half of foreign liabilities. Similarly, Chile's asset position was also the largest at 80 percent of GDP among the group of countries considered. Foreign direct investment abroad accounted for a quarter of Chilean assets abroad and was, by a significant margin, the largest share of GDP from the sample.

Sound Macroeconomic Policies

The resumption of large external inflows in the early 1990s posed a major challenge for policymakers to create a policy framework to reduce the risks of an external credit boom-bust cycle. Through a balanced policy framework, the Chilean authorities sought to harness financial stability to promote financial market development. They responded by implementing conservative monetary and exchange rate policies supported by strong fiscal performance and only a selective and gradual capital account liberalization.

On monetary policy, the framework until the late 1990s aimed at achieving a gradual reduction in inflation while smoothing currency appreciation and building up a significant foreign position. The central bank built on its anti-inflationary credibility by continuously meeting its preannounced inflation tar-

Figure 4.2. International Investment Position
(In billions of U.S. dollars)

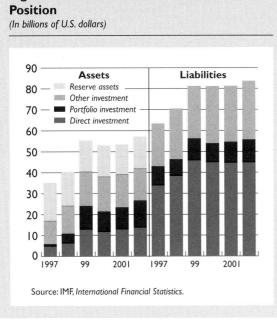

Source: IMF, *International Financial Statistics*.

Figure 4.3. Selected Countries: International Investment Position, 2001
(In percent of GDP)

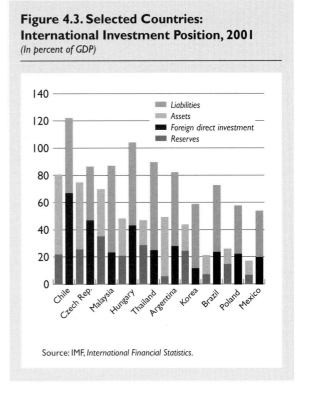

Source: IMF, *International Financial Statistics*.

get. It also managed foreign exchange fluctuations within a reference band and sought to smooth currency appreciation. These policies aimed at avoiding an overvaluation of the currency and allowing conditions for sustained capital inflows in the context of gradual disinflation.

As a by-product of its sterilization and reserve accumulation policy in the 1990s, the central bank became the largest debt issuer and pursued sound debt management (Box 4.1). It actively sought to build a local benchmark yield curve based on an indexed unit of account, the Unidades de Fomento (UF), linked to the consumer price index (CPI). The development of a UF-denominated benchmark yield curve was one of the key factors contributing to the expansion of money markets and private sector fixed-income securities. In addition to nurturing the short end of the curve, the central bank sought to lengthen the duration of its domestic liabilities by issuing long-term paper. By the end of the decade, with the convergence of interest rates to international rates, the bank sought to move away from CPI indexation toward the nominalization of its key monetary instruments and debt issuance at the short end of the yield curve.

To help contain domestic inflationary pressure, in particular in the early 1990s, the authorities also sought to restrict capital flows by adopting a gradual capital account liberalization. The gradual approach sought to differentiate between different types of capital inflows and promote foreign direct invest-

ment. On the one hand, the deregulation of foreign direct investment became a key priority complementing a liberal tax foreign investment law with a gradual easing of limitations on repatriation of profits and capital. On the other hand, other capital flows, including portfolio inflows, were subject to an unremunerated reserve requirement, an implicit tax on capital based on the investment duration. The objective of this requirement was to reduce the country's exposure to volatile flows and to extend the duration of capital inflows.[6]

On fiscal policy, the authorities sought to preserve strong fiscal surpluses to ease the government's debt burden. By 1998, the central government's public debt had fallen to 12.5 percent of GDP from more than 40 percent of GDP a decade earlier. The increased financing needs in the late 1990s led the government to seek finance abroad and set an external benchmark for domestic private issuers.

The government's external debt management has sought to build an external benchmark in a position of financial strength in order to improve external

---

[6]The role and cost-benefit of the capital restrictions in Chile during the 1990s has been a topic of intense debate. See Forbes (2002) and Gallego and Hernandez (2003) for the latest analysis on the costs of these restrictions on firms.

Box 4.1. Establishing Debt Benchmarks in Chile: The Role of the Public Sector

Public debt management has been receiving increased attention in Chile, including with regard to promoting development of financial markets. While the total stock of public debt owed to the domestic private sector has not been rising significantly—it has been broadly stable at around 30 percent of GDP for some time—it is substantial enough for its management to be of consequence, for both the public and private sectors.

To date, the management of public domestic debt has been a task for Chile's central bank, since nearly all such debt is found on its balance sheet. As of end-2002, the central government still had essentially no debt to the domestic private sector, though the Ministry of Finance has indicated that it is considering a domestic bond issue.[1]

In September 2002, the central bank began a program of modernization of its debt management procedures, with these objectives:

- Increasing the liquidity, and facilitating the internationalization, of the domestic fixed-income market;
- Deepening the process of "nominalization" of Chilean financial markets, encouraging the private sector to continue shifting away from use of inflation-indexed instruments;
- Prompting greater capital market efficiency, including development of markets for private debt and hedging instruments.

The bank considered that these moves would serve its broader objectives of deepening and modernizing capital markets and enhancing the economy's integration with Chile's main trading partners.

The specific actions that the central bank took include:

- Following international standards in the design of its debt issues, using "bullet" amortization, and interest paid twice a year;
- Increasing the stock of instruments that would serve as references or benchmarks for debt markets, with a view to establishing a yield curve based on liquid markets for low-risk instruments at various maturities.[2] Following international standards for liquidity, a minimum size for each issue would be US$300 million; and

Composition of Central Bank Paper
(In percent of total)

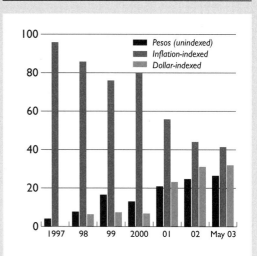

Source: Central Bank of Chile.

- Increasing both the relative share and average maturity of its (nominal) peso debt issues, beginning with a new five-year maturity (previously, the longest maturity of peso issues had been only two years).

These steps build on earlier actions by the central bank that has shifted its liability structure away from inflation-indexed debt in favor of dollar-indexed debt.[3] The greater use of longer-term debt denominated in the domestic currency in particular is widely considered essential in the maturation of emerging market economies and, in particular, reducing their vulnerability to external financial crisis. In that vein, the eventual goal would be to persuade international investors to hold peso-denominated instruments issued by the private sector. Establishing benchmarks, and otherwise promoting the development of the domestic market for such instruments, is seen as a step in that direction.

The bank expects that the reform of its debt structure, by generating a rising volume of intermediation,

---

Prepared by Manmohan Singh.

[1]Domestic debt of the public enterprises is limited mainly to a few recent issues, including by CODELCO and Metro. Subnational governments have no financial debt.

[2]For the time being, the bank is concentrating its new issues at original maturities of two and five years, for both nominal peso and dollar-indexed debt. For inflation-indexed debt, the bank is issuing at maturities of 5, 10, and 20 years.

[3]The greater issuance of peso-denominated debt is part of the bank's "nominalization" strategy, begun in 2001, when the bank switched its operational target from an inflation-indexed interest rate to a simple nominal interest rate.

will allow the market to create new hedging markets for specific risks.

A further benefit of the new debt issues has been the information about inflation expectations now conveyed by interest rate differentials between inflation-indexed and nonindexed debt. On the new five-year issues, such differentials have stayed close to the bank's inflation objective (i.e., to the midpoint of the 2–4 percent target bank).

The size of the central bank balance sheet creates the opportunity to create a considerable range of benchmarks—not only at different maturities, but also in different currency denominations/indexations. Looking forward, the supply of total public domestic debt is not expected to grow very significantly via fiscal deficits, given the government's commitment to fiscal discipline.[4] Still, simply on the basis of existing central bank debt—on the order of US$20 billion, to be compared to the above-mentioned US$300 million standard for minimum issue size—it is clear that the central bank has the opportunity to provide a considerable range of benchmarks. Of course, at the margin benchmarking in any one instrument type reduces the scope for benchmarking in others.

Going forward, the bank's announced policy is to hold constant the share of dollar-indexed instruments in its debt liabilities.[5] Central bank debt is now divided (in increasingly equal shares) between inflation-indexed peso debt, dollar-indexed peso debt, and nominal peso debt, as shown in the figure. Although the rise in the share of dollar-indexed debt since 1997 may appear as an upward trend, in fact it occurred in three discrete episodes (in 1998, 2001, and 2002), in which the bank's motivation was foreign exchange market intervention rather than benchmarking.

In the last few years, the central bank has reduced the share of inflation-indexed (UF) instruments in its liabilities significantly, by roughly half. This decline has come at the shorter maturities; indeed, all of the central bank's debt having maturity greater than five years continues to be in UF form. This pattern reflects the central bank's deliberate policy of promoting "nominalization" of private balance sheets in general, at the same time recognizing that a market preference for inflation protection will likely persist in long-maturity market seg-

ments (e.g., mortgages and pension savings). Looking forward, the 0–5 year market will be increasingly nominalized while the longer-term issues, from 5 to 20 (and possibly more) years, will be in UF.

The central bank's strategy thus entails the eventual loss of the traditional shorter-term UF benchmarks. Such a change naturally involves some costs, at least during a period of transition. One such area may be the interest rate swap (IRS) market, which is not yet fully developed in Chile. The IRS market is relatively illiquid, as the end of short-dated UF issuance has made the market less complete in the 0–2 year segment, and the UF curve does not provide a continuous reference point to price IRS contracts.[6] Looking forward, further progression of the nominalization process will allow the market to price IRS off the curve for nominal peso debt.

Aspects of the Chilean Market for Foreign Exchange Hedging Instruments

The Chilean market for foreign exchange hedging instruments primarily uses the spot and the NDF (nondeliverable forward) markets.

The market for foreign exchange hedging is fairly liquid, with transactions in the spot and NDF market reportedly reaching daily volumes of US$1.4 billion. Most contracts are valued at US$3–5 million, and monthly demand for corporate hedges tends to be about US$4–6 billion. The usual tenor for foreign exchange hedge contracts is between 90 days and two years with ample liquidity; corporates typically roll over their hedges for a longer duration. Cross-currency swaps are available for up to five years, with typical fixing at 30-day intervals.

In recent years, a significant outside stimulus to the private hedging market has been the central bank's net issuance of dollar-indexed debt. The bulk of this injection was in the second half of 2001, when the stock of such debt rose to more than 7 percent of GDP, from about 2 percent of GDP in the previous year; a further increase, to 9 percent of GDP, occurred in 2002. Both increases were part of periods of exceptional intervention to support the Chilean peso. Looking forward, the bank's announced policy is to hold steady the share of dollar-indexed instruments in its total debt liabilities.

---

[4]The (temporary) deficits permitted under the structural balance rule tend to be moderate in size. Debt issues by the public enterprise sector might play a greater role, though in the past most such debt financing has been from external sources.

[5]Although as always the bank reserves the right to foreign exchange intervention if it identifies exceptional circumstances.

[6]A further indication of illiquidity in the shorter-term UF market is that UF interest rates are not quite as far below nominal peso rates as indicators of inflation expectations would predict. For example, in June 2002, one- and two-year yields on inflation-indexed instruments were only about 240 basis points below yields on nominal peso issues with corresponding maturities. Surveys of inflation forecasts, however, suggested somewhat higher expected inflation rates, closer to 3 percent.

financing conditions to the private sector. In the aftermath of the Asian crisis, the authorities perceived an inadequate assessment of the fundamentals underlying Chilean corporate debt and sought to increase foreign investor research on the country's fundamentals. The sovereign benchmark has helped improve the pricing of external corporate bonds, though issuance of such bonds has not picked up.

Financial Sector Reforms

Financial sector reforms have been key factors allowing the development of financial markets in the 1990s. Following the crisis in the 1980s, the authorities implemented far-reaching reforms to the banking, pension, and insurance sectors, coupled with an aggressive privatization program and modernization of the securities market regulations. These reforms supported by stringent regulation and supervision of financial institutions worked to reduce the risks of boom-bust financial cycles.

The comprehensive banking sector reform implemented in 1986 supported the stability and strong profitability of the sector while allowing moderate credit growth during the 1990s.[7] The reform underscored the need for rigid regulation and strict supervision of banking activities, drawing its lessons from the experience of the collapse of the banking system in the early 1980s. The framework implemented a partial deposit insurance system to allow for market discipline, established strict monitoring of loan provisioning, centralized debtor risk information, provided strict limitations to related lending, and imposed portfolio restrictions to limit exposure to exchange rate, interest rate, and credit risks.

Pension reform initiated in 1980 shaped the development of capital markets, helping to finance the privatization process in the late 1980s and setting the development of a sophisticated domestic investor base. The transition from a pay-as-you-go to a fully funded system together with the austere fiscal policy allowed a stable accumulation of large funds to be invested in private sector assets. The reform sought to protect the interest of the contributors to the system, and imposed tight regulations and supervision on fund managers. Stringent limits on the types of securities and issuers were imposed, based on risk ratings, portfolio diversification, ownership concentration, and other specific criteria. Over the past decade, pension regulation has sought to gradually liberalize portfolio investment limits while improving supervision and competition.

The privatization of companies in key industries in the mid-1980s was also a key element contributing to equity market development. Newly privatized firms in the telecommunications, energy, and banking sectors became the flagship companies of the local stock market. The rapid increase in the equity values of these companies in the early 1990s favored the development of conglomerates and economic groups controlling the privatized firms.[8] A wave of mergers and acquisitions, including the large participation of foreign corporations in the late 1990s, contributed to the increased concentration of capital ownership, a key feature of the capital structure in Chile.

Key changes in securities market legislation have sought to strengthen market infrastructure, improve corporate governance and transparency, and expand the set of institutional investors. Given the large size of the insurance and pension funds, regulatory changes to their portfolio investment necessarily have a significant impact on the local securities markets. In 1994 and 1995, the authorities' efforts to continue improving capital market regulation paid off with the enactment of the Private Pensions Law, the Securities Market Law, and Mutual Fund and Insurance Companies legislations. These laws liberalized pension fund portfolio limits, improved regulations, and added security assets and large infrastructure projects to the list of eligible instruments for pension fund investment.

More recently, the authorities have sought to promote further the development of the domestic capital market. New legislation, including the Public Tender Offer Law (OPA Law) in 2000 and the reform of the Capital Markets Law in 2001, has focused on harnessing corporate governance and transparency while easing the investment restrictions of institutional investors and reducing capital market access cost to small firms. The OPA Law provides for strong guarantees to minority shareholder rights and conditions to strengthen corporate governance. It also allows more flexibility to investment funds and regulates the participation of pension funds in initial public offerings. The Capital Markets Law focuses on improving the liquidity and depth of financial markets while facilitating the access to capital markets of emerging firms.[9]

Sources of Corporate Financing

Main Characteristics of Financing Flows

Domestic bank credit remains the primary source of corporates' outside funding, but domestic bond markets have become increasingly important. Do-

---

[7]See Section V for a more detailed account of developments in the banking sector.

[8]See Walker and Lefort (2002) for a more detailed discussion on the formation of economic groups in Chile.

[9]For more detailed analysis of these reforms, see Cifuentes and others (2002).

Table 4.2. Private Sector Financing Issuance
(In millions of U.S. dollars)

	Domestic			External		
	Equity	Bonds	Banks	Equity	Bonds	Banks
1995	223	69	4,419	224	500	1,606
1996	619	133	5,382	297	2,020	3,688
1997	121	83	6,671	67	1,800	5,295
1998	71	798	6,820	—	1,063	3,600
1999	—	745	6,522	—	760	6,181[1]
2000	—	1,252	6,221	—	300	4,764
2001	—	2,739	5,545	—	886	2,074
2002	—	1,732	5,068	—	40	1,061

Sources: Capital One; Superintendency of Securities and Insurance; and Central Bank of Chile.
[1]In 1999, external bank borrowing by Enersis alone accounted for US$3.5 billion.

mestic corporate bond issuance before 1998 represented less than 1 percent of total corporate debt issuance. Yet, by 2001, the annual issuance had reached a quarter of total debt financing. Meanwhile, domestic commercial bank credit to the corporate sector saw a sharp increase from 1995 to 1999. During the period, it doubled in nominal terms and came to account for more than half of total corporate financing (Table 4.2).

In contrast to the increasing domestic debt financing, the corporate sector's external debt financing has seen a pronounced drop since 1997. From 1995 through 1997, external borrowing amounted to almost 50 percent of total corporate sector financing. In contrast, by 2002, the share of external borrowing represented less than 20 percent. External bond financing declined the most as the three-year moving average of bond issuance in 2002 was more than two-thirds down from its 1999 level. The retrenchment of foreign bank financing was also significant, as the three-year moving average dropped by half in the same period.[10]

Equity financing was the main casualty of the emerging market financial turmoil of the late 1990s. New American Depository Receipt (ADR) placements dried up completely after 1998 from a peak of US$755 million in 1994. Similarly, after 1997, there were no new initial public offerings in the local stock market. This is not surprising, given the sharply rising cost of capital in the late 1990s. Using the book-to-market ratio as a rough proxy for the

cost of capital, the cost of issuing equity in 1998–2001 was twice that of the 1992–95 period. The fact that ex post dividend yields were not significantly different between these two periods would suggest that investors were demanding higher risk premia, and discounting share prices accordingly.

The surge in domestic bond market issuance is not a phenomenon unique to Chile, as most emerging market countries experienced a similar expansion (Table 4.3). In fact, domestic issuance for the sample of emerging market countries considered in Figure 4.4 grew almost tenfold from 1997 to 2001, making it the single most important source of financing in 2001 for these countries. However, the pattern of corporate funding showed important regional differences. While domestic bank lending in Asia and Eastern Europe remained the largest source of corporate finance during the period, Latin America experienced a sharp bank retrenchment in 2001 compensated by a large domestic bond issuance. In the case of Chile, however, the financially strong domestic banks continued to issue new loans, albeit at a much lower rate, even as external bank lending fell.

Features of Chilean Corporate Debt

Despite the central bank's nominalization of the key reference interest rate in 2001 and its recent efforts to create a peso-denominated yield curve benchmark, CPI-based indexation in Chile remains pervasive in domestic financial markets. More than 90 percent of fixed-income securities issued from 2000 to 2001 were UF-denominated (i.e., indexed to the CPI), while about half of bank loans were also CPI linked. On the other hand, indexation to the U.S. dollar for domestic fixed-income securities remains low, underscoring the role of local markets as a fi-

---

[10]Note that more than half of the foreign bank borrowing in 1999 was accounted for by the US$3.5 billion external loan to Enersis to finance its investments in Argentina and Brazil, as well as in Chile.

Table 4.3. Domestic Corporate Bond Market
(In billions of Chilean pesos)

	New Issues		Amount Issued		Indebted Entities		Stock Outstanding		Stock in Percent of GDP	
	Private	Public	Private	Public	Private	Public	Private	Public	Private	Public
1995	5	0	28	0	44	2	900	81	3.1	0.3
1996	4	1	57	17	45	2	888	95	2.8	0.3
1997	6	1	36	9	41	1	778	59	2.2	0.2
1998	6	1	377	5	40	1	1,003	65	2.7	0.2
1999	12	1	393	5	43	1	1,287	71	3.5	0.2
2000	20	1	717	12	43	1	2,013	73	5.0	0.2
2001	36	4	1,793	108	62	2	3,832	203	8.8	0.5
2002	35	5	1,245	175	66	4	4,851	463	10.6	1.0

Source: Superintendency of Securities and Insurance.

nancing alternative to shield from increasing foreign exchange volatility.

Another prominent feature of Chile's securities markets is the long duration of the instruments. The average duration of corporate bonds was seven years in 2002 with maturities ranging up to 30 years. The long maturities of bonds reflect the predominant role of pension funds and insurance companies. Given the long duration of pension and life insurance lia-

bilities, these investors represent a readily available source of demand for securities with maturities of 20 or more years. In contrast, as shown in Table 4.4, the average maturity of commercial bank loans was less than two years (partly as a consequence of regulations limiting banks' maturity mismatch).

Investor Base in Chile

The Dominant Role of Contractual Savings Institutions

The large presence of pension funds and insurance companies in the financial system in Chile stems from the enormous growth of these industries since the financial sector reforms in the 1980s. Total assets held by these two industries reached 75 percent of GDP in 2002 with the pension fund assets representing 58 percent of GDP. Excluding equity assets, pension funds and securities firms accounted for almost half of total financial assets outstanding in 2002. At end-2002, pension funds held 39 percent of government bonds, 50 percent of mortgage bonds, 37 percent of corporate bonds, and 35 percent of time deposits (Table 4.5).

This dominant role has helped shape the composition of corporate bond market issuance. The growth of contractual savings has led to a reallocation of savings toward long-term assets to match the long-term maturity of liabilities. This preference for long-term assets has contributed to an increased demand for public and private sector long-term bonds. Correspondingly, corporate firms have responded by issuing bonds in two tranches, one of 8–10 years targeted to pension funds and the other of 20 years or more targeted to insurance companies. Similarly, pension funds and insur-

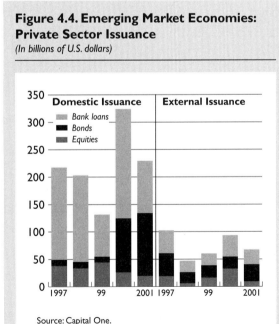

Figure 4.4. Emerging Market Economies: Private Sector Issuance
(In billions of U.S. dollars)

Source: Capital One.
Note: Emerging market economies: Argentina, Brazil, Chile, China, the Czech Republic, Hong Kong SAR, Hungary, Korea, Malaysia, Mexico, Poland, Singapore, and Thailand.

Table 4.4. Private Debt and Issuance Characteristics
(Average maturity; in years)

	Commercial Bank Loans	Domestic Bonds	External Bonds	External Loans
1997	1.2	13.8	33.0	6.3
1998	1.1	17.7	9.5	4.0
1999	1.3	12.1	8.6	2.8
2000	1.6	13.6	10.0	6.1
2001	1.8	14.3	15.1	3.5

Sources: Superintendency of Securities and Insurance; Superintendency of Banks and Financial Institutions; and Capital One.

ance companies induced the development of mortgage bonds with long maturities.

While contributing to the growth of financial markets in Chile during the 1990s, pension and life insurance sectors have been subject to restrictions regarding the composition of their portfolios. As shown in Table 4.6, pension funds and insurance companies have continued to hold a significant share of their assets in public debt—in particular, central bank paper—and bank-intermediated instruments. At end-2001, they held only 20 percent of their portfolio in corporate sector securities. Until the mid-1990s, pension funds could not invest abroad. Since 1995, this restriction has been progressively eased, and, in response, investment in foreign assets has grown considerably, reaching 13 percent of their total portfolio in 2002. More recently, the ceiling on foreign investment by pension funds was raised to 25 percent of pension funds' portfolio.

From early on, the authorities imposed a tight regulation on the type of assets the funds could invest in with the paramount rationale of preserving safety. This regulation has taken the form of maximum limits on holdings of particular classes of instruments. More recent regulatory changes have introduced greater flexibility on the range of instruments allowed; funds initially had been largely restricted to government securities, financial sector securities, and high-grade corporate securities.

Key elements of pension regulation and incentives have also led to the concentration of the fund industry. The combination of the "one fund per Pension Fund Administrators (AFP)" system and the minimum/maximum relative profitability rules (prior to the regulatory changes in 2002), resulted in AFPs having extremely similar portfolio. As evidenced in the literature,[11] the dispersion of returns among

competing pension funds had been very small, favoring a consolidation process that saw the number of pension funds drop from 21 in 1994 to 8 in 1998.

The creation of the multifund system in 2002 is helping to increase investment diversification. Prior to the regulatory changes in 2002, AFPs were only allowed to invest up to 37 percent of their portfolio in shares and were limited to a maximum of 7 percent of an issuer's equity. Since September 2002, AFPs have been allowed to offer five different investment funds (named A through E) with different risk profiles, and investment limits. The restrictions on equity holdings now range from up to 70 percent in Fund A to no equity investment in Fund E. Limits on holdings of individual stocks also vary according to the related ownership of the issuer, liquidity, ownership concentration, and risk classification.

The low participation of pension funds in the equity market also reflects the changing investment conditions in the 1990s. The drop in pension funds' investment in local equity follows from the large tender offers by foreign companies that took over control of large local firms.[12] Similarly, the low return on equity investment in the late 1990s also explains the reduced appetite of pension funds.

While the presence of AFPs has been a key factor contributing to the development of the corporate bond market, pension funds also face important limitations in this market. They can subscribe to a maximum of 20 percent of any bond issue that has to be conducted through open purchases, thus restricting their participation in other placements. As in the case of equity holdings, AFPs are not allowed to invest in bonds rated below investment grade. As a result, market access by potential issuers becomes a yes-no

[11]See Walker and Lefort (2002).

[12]Agosin and Pastén (2003) provide a detailed account of the much discussed Chispas case involving the tender offer for Enersis, Chile's electricity flagship company, by Endesa Spain.

Table 4.5. Share of Pension Funds in Financial Markets and Size of Markets

	Government Debt		Time Deposits		Mortgage Bonds		Corporate Bonds		Equity	
	Size (In billions of U.S. dollars)	AFP (Percent share)	Size (In billions of U.S. dollars)	AFP (Percent share)	Size (In billions of U.S. dollars)	AFP (Percent share)	Size (In billions of U.S. dollars)	AFP (Percent share)	Size (In billions of U.S. dollars)	AFP (Percent share)
1995	25.8	38.9	15.4	8.8	6.1	65.4	2.2	60.3	71.2	10.5
1996	27.1	42.7	18.7	6.2	7.5	65.3	2.1	61.4	65.8	10.5
1997	29.9	40.8	22.3	14.7	9.3	56.0	1.8	57.2	71.8	9.7
1998	28.0	45.4	24.7	17.2	9.0	57.1	2.1	55.3	51.8	8.7
1999	27.3	44.0	24.2	23.1	9.2	56.6	2.4	53.8	68.3	6.0
2000	27.9	46.0	24.4	27.6	9.1	56.6	3.5	41.3	59.7	6.7
2001	27.0	45.9	22.2	28.0	8.6	53.4	5.8	37.3	56.4	6.2
2002	27.3	39.4	22.0	34.6	8.0	49.8	6.8	37.5	48.6	6.7

Sources: Ministry of Finance; Central Bank of Chile; Bloomberg; Superintendency of Securities and Insurance; and Superintendency of Pension Fund Administrators (AFPs).

Table 4.6. Pension Fund Administrators and Insurance Industry Investment Portfolio

	1995	1996	1997	1998	1999	2000	2001	2002
	(In millions of U.S. dollars)							
Total	32,539	36,007	40,722	41,629	45,703	48,176	47,830	48,198
Government paper	12,814	14,846	15,987	16,624	15,615	16,333	15,119	13,058
Financial sector	7,549	9,148	12,288	13,339	15,568	17,192	15,771	16,427
Of which: mortgage paper	5,302	6,673	7,476	7,672	7,981	8,086	7,283	6,537
Of which: time deposits	1,552	1,435	3,474	4,501	5,823	6,980	6,463	7,833
Corporate sector	11,008	10,457	10,293	7,804	7,614	8,179	9,567	10,070
Of which: stocks	8,204	7,514	7,557	4,881	4,510	4,407	3,915	3,548
Of which: bonds	2,077	2,001	1,644	1,885	2,069	2,762	4,679	5,604
Foreign investment	60	175	458	1,889	4,853	4,156	5,027	6,121
Other	1,108	1,381	1,697	1,974	2,053	2,317	2,346	2,522
	(In percent of portfolio)							
Total	100.0	100.0	100.0	100.0	100.0	100.0	100.0	100.0
Government paper	39.4	41.2	39.3	39.9	34.2	33.9	31.6	27.1
Financial sector	23.2	25.4	30.2	32.0	34.1	35.7	33.0	34.1
Of which: mortgage paper	16.3	18.5	18.4	18.4	17.5	16.8	15.2	13.6
Of which: time deposits	4.8	4.0	8.5	10.8	12.7	14.5	13.5	16.3
Corporate sector	33.8	29.0	25.3	18.7	16.7	17.0	20.0	20.9
Of which: stocks	25.2	20.9	18.6	11.7	9.9	9.1	8.2	7.4
Of which: bonds	6.4	5.6	4.0	4.5	4.5	5.7	9.8	11.6
Foreign investment	0.2	0.5	1.1	4.5	10.6	8.6	10.5	12.7
Other	3.4	3.8	4.2	4.7	4.5	4.8	4.9	5.2

Sources: Superintendency of Securities and Insurance; and Superintendency of Pension Fund Administrators.

Table 4.7. Mutual Fund Investment, December 2002
(In millions of U.S. dollars, unless otherwise indicated)

	Fixed Income		Equity	Mixed	Other
	Short term	Medium term			
Number of funds					
National	55	34	27	7	8
International	13	32	57	40	1
Value of funds					
National	3,524	2	81	165	36
International	469	1	56	66	5

Source: Association of Mutual Funds.

matter, based on whether the risk assessment on the quality of the supplied asset is above investment grade. In this regard, given the dominant market presence of the pension funds and insurance companies, market demand is skewed toward high-quality issuers.

Nonetheless, the presence of these institutional investors also has important positive externalities. Walker and Lefort (2002) find evidence that pension reform facilitates the accumulation of "institutional capital" through an adaptive legal framework and increased specialization in the investment decision-making process. The presence of these investors also promotes transparency and integrity through the mandatory risk-taking process and strengthening of corporate governance by promoting minority shareholder interests.

Other Investors

Despite their small size, mutual funds and retail investors also play an important role in capital markets by increasing liquidity, especially at the short range of the bond market. In particular, mutual funds have seen an important rise in their portfolio holdings from less than 4 percent of GDP in 1995 to more than 10 percent in 2002. Table 4.7 shows that mutual fund investment is largely concentrated on the short-term end of fixed-income liabilities. More significantly, the diversity of the funds has contributed to market liquidity at the short-term range of the fixed-income market, especially for central bank paper.

The presence of foreign investors has largely been associated with the development of ADRs in the early and mid-1990s, but has experienced a significant retrenchment ever since. By end-1996, total ADR holdings were significant, at US$6.4 billion. More than 60 percent of firms included in the stock market (IPSA) index were cross-listed as ADRs in

the United States. The preference of ADRs by foreign investors was likely related to higher liquidity and better information and disclosure practices.[13] Nonetheless, despite the suspension of capital controls and elimination of capital gains taxes for foreign investors, the presence of international investors has fallen as reflected by the sharp drop in ADR holdings since 1996.

Challenges for the Development of Domestic Capital Markets

Equity Market Liquidity

Despite Chile's high equity market capitalization, equity turnover is low compared with that of other bourses in the region. As shown in Table 4.8, equity turnover in Chile is well below that of other countries in the region even though Chile's degree of financial development compares favorably to the sample countries.[14] More significant, the equity turnover ratio remains below its peak in 1995 and has continued to decline in recent years (Table 4.9). It is important to note, however, that traded volumes tend to be low when returns are low and when overall economic activity slows down. Hence, the economic slowdown following the Asian crisis could partly explain the lower traded volumes.

Taxation could be another factor affecting stock market liquidity. Cifuentes and others (2002) note that the applications of taxes on the secondary markets of ADRs in 1995 could have contributed to the

---

[13]Cross-listed firms go through the mechanics of standardizing accounting practices and information disclosure on a regular and timely basis.

[14]See Beck, Demirgürç-Kunt, and Levine (2000).

Table 4.8. Latin America: Liquidity in Fixed-Income and Equity Markets

	Equity		Fixed Income	
	Market capitalization (In percent of GDP)	Turnover (In percent)	Transactions (In billions of U.S. dollars)	Turnover (In percent)
Argentina	11	28	17	600
Brazil	19	83	109	...
Chile	84	10	62	274
Colombia	13	18	35	...
Mexico	32	47	1	33

Source: Inter-American Federation of Securities Markets.

drop in liquidity in domestic markets. Yet, these taxes were temporary, as all controls on capital flows were phased out beginning in 1998 and completely eliminated in 2001. Nonetheless, high marginal income tax rates and capital gains taxes created a bias against the domestic stock market in the case of retail and foreign residents. In this regard, the capital market reform in 2001 eliminated the tax on capital gains for high-turnover stocks and short sales of stocks. Yet despite these changes, equity market liquidity did not experience a significant improvement in 2002.

Fixed-Income Market Liquidity

Liquidity in fixed-income markets is significantly higher than that in equities, but it is largely driven by transactions in central bank paper and mortgage bonds. As shown in Table 4.9, fixed-income transactions also fell noticeably in 1999 and 2000, which could also be explained by lower economic activity. Another potential factor is the changing composition of central bank paper over the past three years as the importance of inflation-indexed bonds fell relative to U.S. dollar-linked and nominal paper.

The buy-and-hold investment bias of institutional investors together with increased concentration in the pension and insurance industries could also help explain the low liquidity in bond markets. As shown earlier, these investors play a dominant role in the bond market. The process of pension fund and insurance company consolidation coincided with the drop in bond transactions. Cifuentes and others (2002) show the relationship between rising measures of concentration in the pension fund and banking industry with the downturn in transactions.[15]

---
[15]The paper shows the Herfindahl index for both the pension fund and banking industry increasing since 1995.

More recently, however, corporate bond market transactions have seen a large increase as bond financing has grown rapidly. The low interest rates and recent legal changes have favored this development. In particular, the capital market reform in 2001 has introduced greater flexibility in accessing capital markets and has introduced the possibility of issuing commercial paper for short-term financing by limiting the application of stamp taxes. Relaxation of portfolio limits for mutual and investment funds have also increased activity at the short-term range of corporate bonds.

High Ownership Concentration

The high degree of ownership concentration remains a main feature determining the structure of corporate finance and characteristics of capital markets given its implications for corporate governance and minority shareholder protection (Table 4.10). Recent studies by Lefort and Walker (2000) and Agosin and Pastén (2003) note the prevalence of economic groups, which account for 91 percent of total assets of nonfinancial firms registered in the Superintendency of Securities and Insurance (SVS). Lefort and Walker show that firms affiliated to conglomerates obtain a higher proportion of outside finance and get significantly more long-term debt financing than nonaffiliated firms. They find that controlling shareholders tend to have more equity than strictly needed for control, suggesting that the inside cost of finance for the conglomerates is lower than the cost of outside financing.

Compared with other emerging market countries, the investor concentration in equity markets in Chile remains noteworthy and could explain the low participation of international investors. Figure 4.5 uses a measure of "free float" of outstanding equity, which is the proportion of the outstanding equity market available for purchase in the open market by

Table 4.9. Liquidity in Fixed-Income and Equity Markets
(In millions of U.S. dollars, unless otherwise indicated)

| | Equity | | Fixed Income | | | |
| | | | Total | | Of which: private sector bonds | |
	Transactions	Turnover (In percent of stock)	Transactions	Turnover (In percent of stock)	Transactions	Turnover (In percent of stock)
1996	8,208	11.5	69,513	323.3	1,906	19.8
1997	7,308	11.1	74,817	334.7	2,708	24.4
1998	4,409	6.1	79,627	336.2	4,353	38.9
1999	6,873	13.2	45,520	198.3	2,971	25.4
2000	6,250	9.2	42,483	185.4	4,927	39.0
2001	4,138	6.9	66,536	274.2	4,987	34.5

Sources: Cifuentes and others (2002); and Inter-American Federation of Securities Markets.

Table 4.10. Chile: Ownership Concentration, 1998

| | Total Assets | | Debt | | Equity | | | | |
| | | | | | Controlling shareholders | | Minority shareholders | | |
Conglomerates	In billions of U.S. dollars	Relative size (In percent)	In billions of U.S. dollars	Percent of assets	In billions of U.S. dollars	Percent of assets	In billions of U.S. dollars	Pension funds (In percent)	ADRs (In percent)
Five largest	37.7	54.0	17.3	46.0	10.7	28.6	9.5	27.8	27.5
Ten largest	49.3	70.0	22.1	44.9	15.2	30.8	11.9	32.0	28.0
Twenty largest	57.5	82.0	26.3	45.7	17.6	30.5	13.7	26.6	25.8
All conglomerates	63.9	91.0	29.8	46.7	19.4	30.4	14.6	26.5	24.4
Nonaffiliated	6.1	9.0	2.5	42.7	3.2	53.6			
Total	70.0	100.0	32.5	46.4	22.6	32.4			

Source: Lefort and Walker (2000).

international investors.[16] Chile's free-float measure is among the lowest when compared with other emerging market countries.

The high degree of ownership concentration raises questions about the relative depth of the capital markets and the effectiveness of corporate governance. Agosin and Pastén (2003) argue, however, that the existence of well-developed institutional investors has provided an important counterweight to controlling investors. These investors have played an impor-

tant role of monitoring controllers and limiting rent seeking. While the low turnover of equity reflects the degree of ownership concentration, these institutional investors could be a factor to increase transparency in corporate governance.

The new OPA Law enacted in 2000 has been an important step to strengthen corporate governance. The new framework for public tender offers aims at increasing protection of minority shareholders' rights and reducing rent extraction from controllers. It requires public tender offers to be made open to all shareholders for shares of a large or controlling percentage of a company's shares. The law also attempts to minimize insider agency problems through independent auditing committees with ample powers of oversight over corporate activities. In addition to

---

[16]The non-free-float shares include shareholdings by the government and affiliated entities, corporate treasurers, banks, principal officers, and board members of firms, including shares owned by individuals or families that are related to the company.

Figure 4.5. Selected Countries: Free-Float Measure[1]
(In percent of outstanding equity)

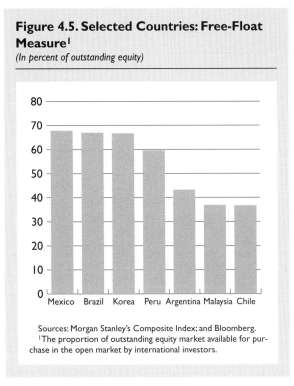

Sources: Morgan Stanley's Composite Index; and Bloomberg.
[1]The proportion of outstanding equity market available for purchase in the open market by international investors.

attempting to improve corporate governance and promoting minority shareholders' rights, the new law has also sought to affect financial deepening by allowing more flexibility to investment funds and regulating the participation of pension funds in public tender offers.

Concluding Remarks

This section has identified important challenges for the development of Chile's domestic capital markets. In particular, low liquidity in equity and bond markets as well as a high degree of ownership concentration remain important impediments. Given the structure of the domestic investor base, the dominant presence of pension funds and insurance companies with buy-and-hold investment strategies helps explain the reduced liquidity. More importantly, the high ownership concentration remains an important feature determining the corporate finance structure and characteristics of capital markets.

Recent changes in financial regulation and legislation, however, have sought to address concerns on the relative depth of capital markets and effectiveness of corporate governance while improving capital market regulation. The OPA Law in 2000 aimed to increase the protection of minority shareholders' rights and tightened corporate governance standards. The Capital Market Reform I enacted in 2001 included tax and

regulatory measures to promote market liquidity, improve firms' market access to finance, and encourage voluntary savings to increase the depth of capital markets. The creation of a multifund pension system is also helping to increase investment diversification. The most recent legislative proposal advancing the second stage of capital market reforms seeks to foster the development of the local venture capital industry as well as tighten market regulation.

Policymakers have thus been actively working to improve financial market infrastructure, tightening corporate governance standards and market regulation. As demonstrated by the recent reforms, the authorities have underscored the role of bridging missing markets, promoting liquidity and transparency, and providing incentives to widen access to investment resources. At least two important broad challenges remain: the internationalization of the investor base and the optimal portfolio allocation of pension and insurance companies while guaranteeing their investment safety.

Higher participation of foreign investors in domestic markets would foster market development, increase investment resources, and allow higher risk diversification. The presence of international investors would help promote the development of new financial instruments and could increase market resilience to external shocks by reducing the balance sheet effects of currency mismatch for domestic companies. While there is no magic policy to ensure foreign investor participation, developed countries' experiences underscore the importance of continuously improving financial market infrastructure and safeguarding investors' rights.

The optimal portfolio allocation of contractual savings, bearing the trade-off between investment efficiency and safety, remains a major policy challenge. Recent changes in regulations have progressively eased investment restrictions of pension and insurance companies and are helping improve the efficiency of domestic capital markets. The difficult policy question ultimately leans on the role of contractual savings in promoting capital market development while preserving the safety of these investments.

References

Agosin, M., and E. Pastén, 2003, "Corporate Governance in Chile," Central Bank of Chile Working Paper No. 209 (Santiago: Central Bank of Chile).

Beck, T., A. Demirgüç-Kunt, and R. Levine, 2000, "A New Database on the Structure and Development of the Financial Sector," *World Bank Economic Review*, Vol. 14, No. 3 (September), pp. 597–605.

Caballero, R., 2002, "Coping with Chile's External Vulnerability: A Financial Problem," in *Economic Growth:*

Sources, Trends, and Cycles, ed. by N. Loayza and R. Soto (Santiago: Central Bank of Chile).

Catalan, M., G. Impavido, and A. Musalem, 2000, "Contractual Savings or Stock Market Development: Which Leads?" Policy Research Working Paper No. 2421 (Washington: World Bank).

Cifuentes R., J. Desormeaux, and C. González, 2002, "Capital Markets in Chile: From Financial Repression to Financial Deepening," Economic Policy Paper No. 4 (Santiago: Central Bank of Chile).

Eyzaguirre, N., and F. Lefort, 1999, "Capital Markets in Chile, 1985–97," in *Chile: Recent Policy Lessons and Emerging Challenges*, ed. by G. Perry and D. Leipziger (Washington: World Bank).

Forbes, K., 2002 "One Cost of the Chilean Capital Controls: Increased Financial Constraints for Smaller Firms," (unpublished; Cambridge, Massachusetts: Massachusetts Institute of Technology).

Gallego, F., and N. Loayza, 2001, "Financial Structure in Chile: Macroeconomic Development and Microeconomic Effects," in *Financial Structure and Economic Growth: A Cross-Country Comparison of Banks, Markets, and Development,* ed. by A. Demirgüç-Kunt and R. Levine (Cambridge, Massachusetts: MIT Press).

Gallego, F., and L. Hernandez, 2003, "Microeconomic Effects of Capital Controls: The Chilean Experience During the 1990s," Central Bank of Chile Working Paper No. 203 (Santiago: Central Bank of Chile).

International Monetary Fund, 2002, "Emerging Equity Markets," Chapter IV in *Global Financial Stability Report,* World Economic and Financial Surveys (Washington, June).

Holland, S., and F. Warnock, 2003, "Firm-Level Access to International Capital Markets: Evidence from Chilean Equities," *Emerging Markets Review,* Vol. 4, No. 1 (March), pp. 39–51.

Lefort, F., and E. Walker, 2000, "Ownership and Capital Structure of Chilean Conglomerates: Facts and Hypotheses for Governance," *ABANTE,* Vol. 3, No. 1, pp. 3–27.

Levine, R., and M. Carkovic, 2002, "Finance and Growth: New Evidence and Policy Analyses for Chile," Central Bank of Chile Working Paper No. 157 (Santiago: Central Bank of Chile).

Walker, E., and F. Lefort, 2002, "Pension Reform and Capital Markets: Are There Any (Hard) Links?" Social Protection Discussion Paper No. 0201 (Washington: World Bank).

V   The Chilean Banking System: Recent Developments

Marco A. Espinosa-Vega

This section provides a brief update of the Chilean banking system by reporting recent developments and regulatory changes, standard prudential indicators, and the view of rating agencies. It also discusses the recent Inverlink affair, focusing on the preemptive liquidity measures taken by the authorities after this incident of fraud came to light.

Structure and Activities of the Banking System

As of December 2002, the Chilean banking system held about US$63.2 billion in assets or about 100 percent of GDP—including about US$44.5 billion in loans and US$12.3 billion in negotiable financial instruments.

The structure of the banking system continues to evolve. Currently the system consists of 26 banks, including 7 branches of foreign banks and the government-owned bank (Banco Estado). During 2002, two new banks (Banco Ripley and Banco HNS) entered the system. Early in 2003, the only remaining finance company or consumer credit agency (Financiera Conosur, with 53 branches throughout the country) became a full-fledged commercial bank (Banco Conosur).

During 2002, the total bank loan portfolio continued to grow in tandem with economic activity. Consumer loans[1] have shown the strongest performance with a 12 percent (year-on-year) growth rate in real terms. Mortgage lending grew at 6 percent (year-on-year) in real terms while commercial lending stayed flat—due in part to alternative financing sources available to large firms.

There has been a shift in the composition of banks' assets, as well as in their deposits and loans. Since the announcement in 2001 of the central bank's "nominalization" of its monetary policy operations there has been a shift in the composition of banks' assets (Figure 5.1), deposits, and loans from inflation-indexed (denominated in Unidad de Fomento (UF))[2] to nonindexed instruments.

Banks have not been heavily involved in underwriting and securitization, even though the 1997 amendment to the 1986 banking law permits such activities. Banks' involvement in the derivatives market is dominated by currency hedging. Banks participate actively in foreign exchange forwards and swaps.

A long-standing characteristic of the Chilean banking system, its relatively low levels of dollarization, continues to hold (Figure 5.2). Since early 2002, dollarization ratios have been essentially flat (for deposits) or have tended to decline slightly (for loans).[3]

The banking system appears fairly concentrated. The 10 largest banks account for some 85 percent of deposits and loans, and the 2 largest banks represent almost half of the system's deposits. Such concentration might raise concerns of possible anticompetitive practices and increased systemic risk. However, recent studies find that Chile does not stand out as having a particularly concentrated banking system, that this concentration so far has not adversely affected the degree of competition, and that larger banks are not associated with riskier practices in Chile.[4]

The system also continues to have significant foreign participation. Foreign-owned or controlled banks' assets account for 44 percent of banking system's assets. Recent cross-country research associates the presence of foreign banks with the import of sound risk management systems developed by head offices with advanced financial and banking markets, and with increased efficiency of domestic banks.[5] In some countries, there has been concern that entry of foreign banks could eliminate the small

---

[1]The system's technology to evaluate consumers' creditworthiness is fairly strong. The local credit bureau (DICOM) is owned by Equifax.

[2]The UF is a unit of account that indexes the principal of financial contracts and transactions to the previous month's inflation rate.

[3]Earlier, the 4- to 5-point rise in dollarization ratios seen from January to October of 2001 was associated partly with a 23 percent depreciation of the Chilean peso against the U.S. dollar, rather than a significant flow increase.

[4]See Levine (2000) and Chumacero and Langoni (2001).

[5]See Barajas (2000) and Claessens and others (1998).

Figure 5.1. Nominal Versus Inflation-Indexed Loans and Deposits
(In percent of total)

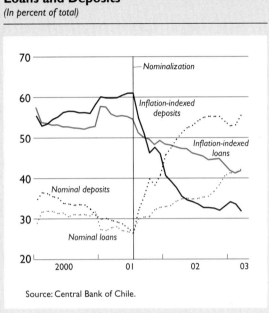

Source: Central Bank of Chile.

Figure 5.2. Dollarization of the Banking System
(In percent of total)

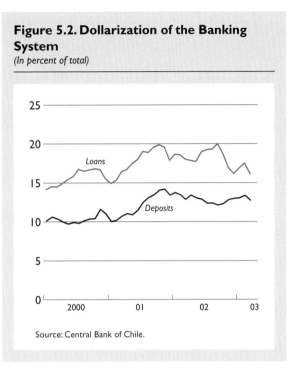

Source: Central Bank of Chile.

local banks that normally cater to low-income consumers; however, there is no empirical evidence to support this claim.[6] In addition, in Chile, the Banco Estado ensures the provision of banking services to all regions of the country through its widespread branch network, maintains a large volume of passbook savings accounts, and makes a substantial amount of consumer and mortgage loans including to low-income households.[7]

Recent Changes in Banking Regulation and Supervision

Mortgage refinancing activity has been spurred by the November 2002 approval by congress of the elimination of the "stamp" tax paid on refinancing of home mortgages and by low interest rates.

The central bank is engaged in modernizing the country's payments system. Open market operations already are conducted electronically. By 2004, the central bank will require the electronic custody and trading of all large-denomination assets. Also in 2004, all large-denomination asset transactions will be settled on a real-time gross settlement (RTGS) basis.

In Chile, the central bank and the Superintendency of Banks and Financial Institutions (SBIF) have regulatory powers over the banking system. Since the 2002 Article IV consultation with the IMF, they have taken the following regulatory measures:

- The central bank authorized banks to issue interest-bearing deposit accounts. However, the move has not induced a large switch from noninterest-bearing to interest-bearing accounts—in part due to the low opportunity cost that a low inflationary environment represents for depositors.[8]

- The SBIF issued a new regulation requiring banks to include all loan charges in a single interest rate figure, and to publish interest rates charged on consumer loans periodically. The goal of this increase in transparency was to promote more competition among banks, in particular to induce a higher degree of interest rate pass-through to consumer lending rates.

- The SBIF introduced regulations that would require banks to (1) restrict how much of the net worth of their affiliates could be included in the consolidated balance sheets; (2) obtain previous

---

[6]See, for instance, Clarke and others (2001).

[7]Some of this activity reflects savings deposits and the servicing of subsidized mortgages provided in conjunction with the government's low-income housing programs.

[8]This situation is likely to change when the central bank switches to a tighter mode. Significant increases in sight deposit accounts would represent a larger potential deposit insurance liability for the central bank. In light of this possibility, it might be a good idea to revisit the question of how generous deposit insurance might be.

authorization of the SBIF before selling or charging-off reposed assets; (3) apply their own portfolio risk models for loan provisioning; and (4) meet guidelines for internal auditing committees to bring them up to international best practices by 2004.

Perhaps the most significant of these regulatory changes has been allowing banks to design their own portfolio risk models. The regulation anticipates the new direction of the Basel II Committee's recommendations of moving to greater reliance on banks' internal risk management systems. The SBIF reports that it is training its staff to better understand and evaluate the banks' internal risk models. The SBIF also reports that its risk unit has met with all the risk departments of the different banks to look into the assumptions of the banks' risk models and to ensure consistency between the asset classification and their provisioning.

Risk Management Policies, Prudential Indicators, and Stress Tests

The Chilean banking system continues to enjoy a reputation for soundness, for weathering regional storms, and for an effective provision of credit to the private sector (Box 5.1). The recent collapse of the Argentine banking system and political uncertainties in Brazil had a limited impact on the Chilean banking system.

Overall prudential indicators continue to point to a healthy banking system (Table 5.1). The system continued to be well capitalized during 2002, but there was a slight deterioration in the quality of the banking system's portfolio, and a small decline in the banking system's profits. As shown in Table 5.1, during 2002 the banking system as a whole

- Registered a slight increase in overdue loans;[9]

- Showed a slight decrease in loan loss reserve coverage;

- Maintained a healthy coverage ratio of 129.5 percent as of December 2002;

- Continues to be well capitalized, displaying a small increase in its capital adequacy ratio to 14.01 percent in December 2002; and

- Experienced a small decline over the year in net income after taxes, both as a rate of return on assets and as a rate of return on equity. The most

significant factor in this was the higher costs associated with the mergers of several banks (greater administrative costs and increases in loan loss provision reserves).[10] Nevertheless, the overall profitability of the banking system remains strong and stable.

Even with the favorable prudential indicators just listed, the Chilean banking system could still be exposed to a number of potential shocks. In order to assess the vulnerability of the banking system to some of these shocks, in late 2001 IMF staff conducted a series of stress tests.[11] The tests consisted of applying (1) a hypothetical 25 percent depreciation of the peso to the net foreign exchange rate exposure of each bank; (2) a shock to the central bank bonds yield curve and using a repricing gap model of interest rate risk to analyze the sensitivity to interest rate shocks of the difference between the flow of interest earned by each bank's assets and flow of interest paid on its liabilities; and (3) a credit risk shock by assuming that the share of overdue loans as a percentage of total loans doubled with 100 percent provisioning of the simulated increase. Most banks would have been able to comfortably meet the minimum risk-based capital adequacy requirements after each shock.

The SBIF is considering making this kind of stress analysis part of its routine vulnerability assessment. It is currently engaged in an updated, similar stress-testing exercise, and expects to release its findings.

Preemptive Liquidity Measures: The Aftermath of the Inverlink Affair

A case of fraud of some significance, involving a financial holding company, emerged in March 2003. Although this case originated outside the banking system, its repercussions soon extended to the banking system.

In early March, a bribed official at CORFO (a second-tier development bank, under the supervision of the Ministry of Economy) was discovered to have handed over more than US$100 million in government-owned securities to Inverlink, a private financial holding company, which had then recently sold them in the secondary market. Only a few weeks earlier, Inverlink—whose interests included a mutual fund, an insurance company, and a pension fund—had been caught bribing a central bank employee to deliver confidential information.

---

[9]Chile differs from Generally Accepted Accounting Procedures (GAAP) accounting practices regarding overdue loans. Only the portion of loan overdue for more than 90 days is classified as overdue, unless legal proceedings are initiated for recovery.

[10]Banco de Chile and Banco Edwards merged in January, and the Santander and Santiago banks merged in August.
[11]For details, see IMF (2002).

Box 5.1. The Credit Allocation Role of Banks in Chile

Since the 1970s Chilean banks have played a key role in the allocation of credit to the private sector. These banks have been the most dynamic in terms of credit allocation in Latin America. For example, at end-2002, bank lending portfolio accounted for 70 percent of GDP compared with less than 30 percent for Brazil. The banking sector has held on to its financial liberalization efforts and has carried out some financial innovations. Factors that have contributed to the prominent role of banks in the allocation of credit include financial liberalization, fiscal discipline, a limited-participation state-owned bank, availability of an inflation-indexed unit of account, a strong technology to evaluate consumers' creditworthiness, privatization of the pension system, and the banking regulatory regime and safety net.

As reported in, for example, Caballero (2001), equity markets saw a rapid expansion in the early 1990s. Also, as reported in Section III, in just the last few years, there has also been a resurgence of domestic bond financing and a retreat from equity markets. However, the importance of bank credit continues to grow (see table).

Relative Importance of Bank Loans

| | Stock as Percent of Total | | |
Source of Financing	1995	1999	2003
Loans	32	41	44
Equity	66	57	49
Bonds	2	2	7

Sources: Superintendency of Banks and Financial Institutions; and Superintendency of Securities and Insurance.

The market for consumer loans and mortgage loans has recently experienced rapid growth. Nevertheless, credit to firms continues to be the largest component of bank credit (Figure A).

Financial liberalization is credited[1] with the takeoff of credit to the private sector observed after the mid-1970s. After years of financial repression, there was a move to drastically reduce reserve requirements, relax deposit and loan interest rate caps, reduce entry barriers, and privatize the banking system. These measures are summarized by Morley and others (1999) in the financial liberalization index presented in Figure B. It is important to mention, however, that as reported in

Section II, the liberalization of the 1970s left some underlying vulnerabilities unaddressed.

Fiscal discipline has meant that commercial banks have not ended up absorbing massive amounts of public debt. The private sector is the main recipient of bank funds. The consolidated government debt represents only 13 percent of the banking system's total assets (Figure C). From a Latin American perspective, Chile is a clear outlier in this regard.

Government participation in the banking system is limited. There is only one state-owned bank, the Banco Estado. Its assets now represent 14 percent of total bank assets (Figure D). The Banco Estado ensures the provision of banking services to all regions of the country through its branch network. It maintains a large volume of passbook savings accounts and makes a substantial amount of low-income housing loans. Quasi-fiscal activity seems to be limited, however, judging by Banco Estado's record of profitability.

A. Composition of Bank Credit by Destination

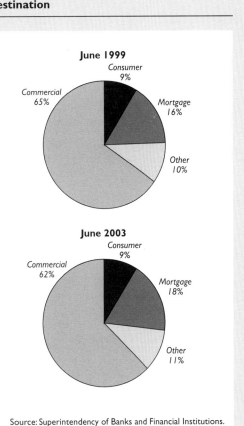

June 1999

Consumer 9%
Commercial 65%
Mortgage 16%
Other 10%

June 2003

Consumer 9%
Commercial 62%
Mortgage 18%
Other 11%

Source: Superintendency of Banks and Financial Institutions.

[1]See, for example, Gallego and Loayza (2000).

Box 5.1 *(concluded)*

B. Bank Credit and Financial Liberalization

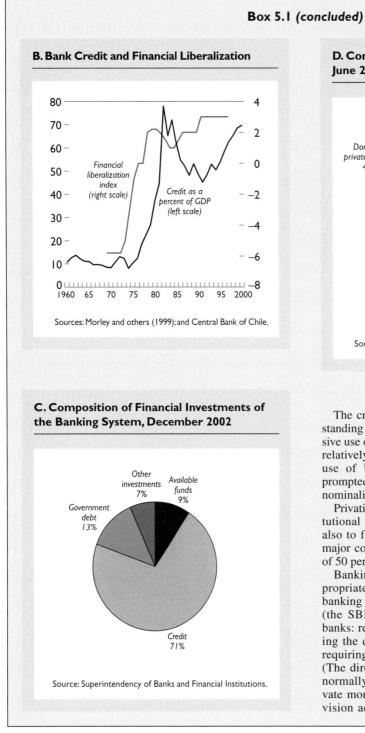

Sources: Morley and others (1999); and Central Bank of Chile.

C. Composition of Financial Investments of the Banking System, December 2002

Source: Superintendency of Banks and Financial Institutions.

D. Composition of Bank Ownership, June 2003

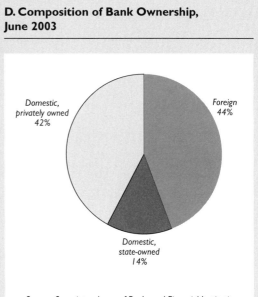

Domestic, privately owned 42%

Foreign 44%

Domestic, state-owned 14%

Source: Superintendency of Banks and Financial Institutions.

The creation of the UF may help explain two long-standing characteristics of Chilean banking: the extensive use of inflation-indexed assets and liabilities, and a relatively low level of dollarization. (Since 2001, the use of UF denomination has declined somewhat, prompted by a change in central bank policy known as nominalization (Figure E).)

Privatization of the pension system created an institutional investor base able to absorb public debt and also to fund banks. Private pension funds, which are major collectors of savings, now hold assets in excess of 50 percent of GDP.

Banking regulation and market discipline seem appropriately balanced. As discussed in Section II, the banking law of 1986 provided the supervisory agency (the SBIF) with new tools to limit risk taking by banks: restriction of business with related parties; rating the quality of banking investments; and in 1997 requiring compliance with Basel capital requirements. (The direction of criticism of Chilean regulation has normally been that it has been too risk-averse.) Private monitoring seems to complement official supervision adequately. Chile has enjoyed a fairly strong

When the theft and subsequent sale of CORFO's financial instruments was discovered on March 7, the Treasury asked the courts to declare an embargo on the payment of the stolen instruments. After finding enough merit on the request, the courts complied

and declared an embargo. Trading in all time deposits soon stopped as the market worked to sort out the holders of the stolen instruments. The holdup on trading of time deposits generated some market uncertainty. A number of mutual funds (most of them

E. Financial System Credit by Currency
(In percent of total)

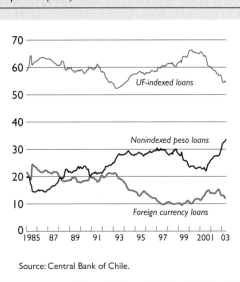

Source: Central Bank of Chile.

F. Composition of Bank Loans by Amount
(In Unidades de Fomento)[1]

August 1999

500–5000
10%

0–500
5%

> 5000
85%

June 2002

500–5000
13%

0–500
12%

> 5000
75%

Source: Superintendency of Banks and Financial Institutions.
[1]In August 1999, 500 UF were worth about US$14,400; in June 2002, 500 UF were worth about US$11,900.

technology to evaluate consumers' creditworthiness DICOM, the local credit bureau, has operated in the country since 1979. In addition, Chile has a system of explicit deposit insurance that according to Budnevich and Franken (2003) and Martinez and Schmukler (2001)is not so generous as to prevent market discipline by depositors.

The credit allocation role of banks in Chile is not yet fully developed. Levine and Carkovic (2002) make the case that the Chilean financial system is not all that it could be, and in fact is less developed than in some other countries with strong growth records. Large corporations are the main beneficiaries of bank credit. Small and medium-sized enterprises still enjoy a relatively minor share of bank credit and are the first to face the brunt of credit crunches and economic downturns. Short-term lending comprises a large percentage of the banks' credit portfolio. An important factor in this is prudential regulation limiting banks' maturity mismatch.

The banks' credit portfolio is dominated by large loans, but the composition has only recently been shifting to smaller loans (Figure F).

bank affiliates) also experienced very significant withdrawals.[12] As a consequence, the liquidity needs

of the banking system increased markedly. In response, during March 10–14, 2003:

- The central bank provided liquidity through its overnight repo window, and swap operations in

---

[12]A reported US$800 million was withdrawn from the mutual funds, out of a total of US$6.2 billion after the scandal broke.

Table 5.1. Financial System Indicators
(In percent)

	December							April
	1996	1997	1998	1999	2000	2001	2002	2003
Solvency								
Effective capital/risk-weighted assets[1]	...	...	12.48	13.53	13.34	12.73	14.01	14.40
Basic capital/total assets[2]	...	...	7.49	7.75	7.51	7.24	7.20	7.38
Credit risks								
Loan loss provisions/total loans	1.34	1.42	1.91	2.55	2.52	2.37	2.36	2.30
Overdue loans/total loans	0.95	0.96	1.45	1.67	1.73	1.62	1.82	1.94
Loan loss provisions/overdue loans	141.1	147.9	131.7	152.7	145.7	146.3	129.5	118.9
Results								
After income/adjusted assets (ROA)[3]	1.14	1.01	0.90	0.73	1.00	1.28	1.04	1.10
After tax income/capital and reserves (ROE)	15.50	13.67	11.54	9.36	12.70	17.70	14.39	14.90
Efficiency								
Operating costs/gross operational margin	66.50	66.45	61.44	60.19	60.76	56.15	55.21	53.92
Operating costs/adjusted assets	3.33	3.19	3.13	2.94	2.84	2.78	2.55	2.58
Foreign exchange risk								
Net open foreign exchange position (percent of capital)[3] (sum of on- and off-balance-sheet exposure)	...	...	...	11.67	4.33	3.58	4.27	4.30

Source: Superintendency of Banks and Financial Institutions.

[1]Effective capital corresponds to basic capital less equity plus the sum of voluntary provisions and subordinated bonds.

[2]Basic capital is equivalent to capital and reserves.

[3]Figure for 2003 is through March.

U.S. dollars with resale agreements. The liquidity provided by the central bank between March 10 and March 14 represented an abrupt increase of about 50 percent in the level of liquidity in the system that, judging by the lack of gap between interbank market interest rates and the bank's unchanged monetary policy rate, appeared adequate;

• Regulators put some Inverlink companies under government administration and their assets in trust;

• The central bank relaxed its redeeming of maturing regulations on deposits in order to provide additional liquidity to the market;

• The SBIF made a public statement about the health of the banking system; and

• The government struck an agreement with the banking community and reversed the stop payment order on the stolen securities pending a decision by the courts on their lawful ownership.

The central bank allowed the liquidity to remain in the system until March 24. In hindsight, the extended liquidity period was more than adequate, judging by the fact that, on average, for this period the interbank rate was 20 basis points below the monetary policy rate. The authorities indicated that the reason for this liquidity excess was to signal the central bank's intent to meet any liquidity needs during the exceptional circumstances. The liquidity excess was gradually removed until its total recall on April 8, 2003.

Looking back, Chile avoided major systemic effects because the banking system as a whole is on a sound footing, because it is vastly larger than the amount of stolen securities (0.15 percent of GDP),[13] and because the central bank and the SBIF intervened swiftly. In the end, the episode did not induce rating agencies to change any of their bank ratings.[14]

Although the CORFO-Inverlink affair has not had a lasting negative effect on the banking system, it did bring to light a number of current and potential problems with the financial system and its supervision:

---

[13]Total assets of the banking system are close to 100 percent of GDP.

[14]See, for instance, Moody's Investor Service (2003).

- The need to institute better public sector financial controls. A recent congressional investigative commission concluded that CORFO lacked basic financial controls, and its financial desk was not implementing existing procedures. The commission also noted that the Controller General had identified problems relevant to the case as far back as 1998, but that these had not been addressed. (It can be noted also that the securities thefts had gone on for some time, yet had gone undetected by several government review procedures; CORFO became aware of the problem only after a private bank suspected irregularities and notified it.)

- The desirability of having electronic custody and trading of assets. The theft of assets from CORFO was facilitated by their being in physical (paper) form. Subsequently, the difficulty of sorting out who was currently holding the paper assets created unnecessary havoc.

- The need to establish better mechanisms for the three supervisory agencies[15] to share information. The SVS oversees all mutual funds but did not have to share information with the SBIF regarding the activities of Inverlink's mutual fund because it did not have a banking interest directly associated with it.

In response, the authorities appended a number of proposals to the capital market reform package that had already been in preparation. Capital Market Reform II is an ambitious set of 60 proposals, recently sent to congress, to either modify old or create new laws. The proposals include

- Regulation, coordination, and modernization changes in the financial system by, for example, allowing the SBIF more discretion in denying bank licenses;

- Allowing more SBIF control over banks' subsidiaries;

- Establishing mechanisms to share information among the three supervisory agencies; and

- Immaterialization and electronic trading of assets.

These measures should help resolve some of the current and potential infrastructure problems in the banking system and its supervision identified above. However, a comprehensive assessment of the remaining and potential problems and their solution would be better addressed in the upcoming Financial Sector Assessment Program.

Grading by Rating Agencies

Ratings agencies continue to see the Chilean banking system as one of the strongest and best regulated in Latin America. For example, in a February 2003 report, Fitch observed that in a second year of regional volatility, Chile continued to differentiate itself from the rest of Latin America. Moody's June 2003 report on the Chilean banking system also provides a positive outlook. This report sees the Chilean banking system as one with sound financial fundamentals.[16] Nevertheless, both reports stress the need for close monitoring in the face of regional and global uncertainties and a slower economy.

Table 5.2 reports the long-term foreign and local currency classifications of individual banks, as of July 2003. This table presents a picture of a stable banking system with the four largest banks displaying some of the best ratings and with most banks assigned a positive outlook.

Concluding Remarks

The Chilean banking system continues to command a reputation for stability and strength. The system has been tested in the last two years by regional uncertainties, slow recovery, and more recently, by a homegrown shock, in the form of the Inverlink case. The system has weathered these shocks well. However, the first type of shocks highlights the importance, as suggested in the Moody's and Fitch reports, for close monitoring. The adoption and improvements of vulnerability assessment techniques of the type discussed above are likely to help analysts in their endeavor.

The shock originating from the Inverlink case highlighted the need for modernization of certain practices and regulations involving transactions and custody of securities in secondary markets. The authorities took swift action and seized the opportunity to add proposals for some of these needed changes to the Capital Markets Reform II program that had been under preparation and is now in congress. Furthermore, the SBIF has started to anticipate the new winds of the Basel II Accord. However, as the globalization process continues, as new financial products become part of the banking landscape, and as the line between banking and other financial sectors continues to blur, regulation and safety net designs will have to adapt flexibly and expeditiously in Chile as elsewhere.

---

[15]The SBIF, the Superintendency of Securities and Insurance (SVS), and the Superintendency of Pension Fund Administrators (SAFP).

[16]See Moody's Investor Service (2003) and Fitch (2003).

Table 5.2. Long-Term Credit Ratings, as of June 2003

	Foreign Currency[1]			Local Currency	
	Fitch	Moody's	Standard & Poor's	Feller	Fitch-Chile
ABN AMRO Bank (Chile)				AA+	AA
Banco BICE		Baa 1 6/3/2003		AA	AA
Banco Conosur				BBB+	BBB+
Banco de Chile	A- 10/18/2002	Baa 1 6/9/2003	A- 11/20/2002	AA+	AA+
Banco de Crédito e Inversiones		Baa 1 6/3/2003		AA	AA
Banco de la Nación Argentina				BB	BB+
Banco del Desarrollo				A-	A
Banco Estado		Baa 1 6/3/2003	A- 9/11/2002[2]	AA+	AA+
Banco do Brasil S.A.				BBB	BBB
Banco Falabella				A+	A+
Banco Internacional				BBB+	A-
Banco Ripley				A-	A-
Banco Santander—Santiago	A- 12/2/2002	Baa 1 6/3/2003	A- 12/13/2002[2]	AA+	AA+
Banco Security				AA-	AA-
Banco Sudameris				A+	AA-
Bank Boston N.A.				AA	AA-
BBVA		Baa 1 6/3/2003		AA-	AA
Citibank N.A.				AA+	AA+
Corpbanca	BBB 12/12/2002[2]	Baa 3 6/3/2003		AA-	AA-
Deutsche Bank Chile				AA+	AA+
Dresdner Bank Lateinamerika				AA	AA
HNS Banco				A-	A-
HSBC Bank Chile				AA+	AA-
JP Morgan Chase Bank				AA+	AA+
Scotiabank Sud Americano		Baa 1 6/3/2003	BBB+ 3/19/2003	A+	AA-
The Bank of Tokyo-Mitsubishi				AA-	AA-

Sources: Fitch; Moody's; Standard & Poor's; Feller Rate; and Fitch-Chile.
[1]Including date of most recent rating change or affirmation.
[2]Positive rating outlook.

References

Bandiera, O., and others, 1999, "Does Financial Reform Increase or Reduce Savings?" World Bank Policy Research Working Paper No. 2062 (Washington: World Bank).

Banking System Outlook, 2003, "Chile: Balance Sheet Management and Productivity Gains Support Earnings and Stable Outlook" (June).

Barajas, A., 2000, "Foreign Investment in Colombia's Financial Sector," in *The Internationalization of Financial Services*, ed. by Steiner and N. Salaza.

Budnevich, C., and H. Franken, 2003, "Disciplina de Mercado en la Conducta de los Depositantes y Rol de las Agencias Clasificadoras de Riesgo: El Caso de Chile," *Economía Chilena*, Vol. 6, No. 2 (August), pp. 45–70.

Caballero, R., 2001, "Coping with Chile's External Vulnerability: A Financial Problem," in *Economic Growth: Sources, Trends, and Cycles*, ed. by N. Loayza and R. Soto (Santiago: Central Bank of Chile).

Chumacero, R., and P. Langoni, 2001, "Riesgo, Tamaño y Concentración en el Sistema Bancario Chileno," *Economía Chilena*, Vol. 4, No. 1 (April), pp. 25–34.

Claessens, S., A. Demirgüç-Kunt, and H. Huizinga, 1998, "How Does Foreign Bank Entry Affect the Domestic Banking Market?" World Bank Policy Research Paper No. 1918 (Washington: World Bank).

Clarke, G., R. Cull, M. Martinez Peria, and S. Sanchez, 2001, "Bank Lending to Small Business in Latin America: Does Bank Origin Matter?" World Bank Policy Research Paper No. 2760 (Washington: World Bank).

Fitch, 2003, "Chilean Banks—End-2002 Results" (February).

Gallego, F., and N. Loayza, 2000, "Estructura Financiera en Chile: Desarrollos Macroeconómicos y Efectos Microeconómicos," *Economía Chilena*, Vol. 3, No. 2 (August), pp. 5–30.

International Monetary Fund, 2002, *Chile: Selected Issues*, IMF Country Report No. 02/163 (Washington: International Monetary Fund).

Levine, R., 2000, "Bank Concentration: Chile and International Comparisons," Central Bank of Chile Working Paper No. 62 (Santiago: Central Bank of Chile).

———, and M. Carkovic, 2002, "Finance and Growth: New Evidence and Policy Analyses for Chile," Central Bank of Chile Working Paper No. 157 (Santiago: Central Bank of Chile).

Martinez Peria, M., and S. Schmukler, 2001, "Do Depositors Punish Banks for Bad Behavior? Market Discipline, Deposit Insurance, and Banking Crises," *Journal of Finance*, Vol. 56, No. 3 (June), pp. 1029–51.

Moody's Investor Service, 2003, "Banking System Outlook: Chile," June.

Morley, S., R. Machado, and S. Pettinato, 1999, "Indexes of Structural Reform in Latin America" (Santiago: UN Economic Commission for Latin America and the Caribbean).

VI An Assessment of Chile's External Position

Rodolfo Luzio

This section reviews Chile's external position, integrating information on the country's international investment position and the structure of external debt.[1,2] The objective is to analyze the possibility of an external liquidity squeeze on the balance of payments as well as to test for potential solvency problems. The approach followed combines the standard IMF debt sustainability analysis framework and alternative tests using newly published data on Chile's international investment position. The analysis focuses on (1) the external debt dynamics; (2) the sensitivity of gross external financing requirements to specific shocks; and (3) the implications of Chile's international investment position for external vulnerability.

The main results underscore the strength of Chile's aggregate external position. We summarize below our key findings.

- Using the standard debt sustainability framework, we see that various hypothetical shocks during 2003 to 2004 would raise the external debt-to-GDP ratio during those years, but would still be consistent with a gradual decline in the debt ratio thereafter. Moreover, although some of the shocks considered would substantially raise the debt ratio for a time, the risks of these standardized shocks seems remote, given the strength of Chile's current policy framework.

- Liquidity problems are not expected given the country's significant international reserve holdings.[3] A drawdown in international reserves would be sufficient to cover Chile's annual gross external financial requirements under all stress tests considered.

- Chile's foreign asset position is a source of strength. Liquid external asset holdings by the private sector were more than sufficient to cover the country's total external financing requirements at end-2001.[4] Foreign direct investment (FDI) in Chile amounted to two-thirds of GDP, helping explain that foreign-owned Chilean resident firms held more than half of Chile's total external debt. Sensitivity analysis using the net international investment position shows the dampening effects of direct investment holdings on the aggregate net liability.

- The sound policy framework, including the credible inflation targeting, foreign exchange free float, and strong fiscal position, should provide enough flexibility to accommodate and support temporary shocks to external financing conditions.

The results derived from an aggregate analysis of vulnerability carry some caveats. In principle, the aggregate approach could mask financial vulnerabilities in specific sectors or business groups that could have amplifying effects with systemic implications (a general problem, not particularly specific to Chile). On the other hand, the analysis relying on traditional residency-based aggregates could also understate potential sources of strength, especially in the case of Chile. In particular, the presence of foreign-owned Chilean resident firms responsible for half of total external debt could be a source of external support, as demonstrated recently by the case of Enersis (Box 6.1). Chile's supportive investment environment with strong property right guarantees is a key reason for the willingness of foreign parent com-

---

[1]This section uses data as of August 2003. Data on Chile's international investment position have been revised since then to reflect more detailed information about the private sector external position, including data on trade credits and other short-term liabilities and assets.

[2]Current work at the Central Bank of Chile, in preparation of a Financial Stability Report, has focused on developing a more detailed and comprehensive assessment of Chile's external position.

[3]The analysis in this section does not refer to the more demanding question of the optimal level of international reserves, but simply seeks to compare the level of reserves with financing needs under various scenarios. To consider the optimal level of international reserves, a more comprehensive analysis of the costs and benefits of liquidity holdings would be required, including the probability of adverse shocks.

[4]Using a narrow definition of liquid assets, which includes only short-term deposits and currency holdings but excludes short-term credits, would indicate that private sector liquid holdings would cover more than two-thirds of the private sector's short-term debt on a residual maturity basis.

Box 6.1. Distress Among Chile's Foreign-Owned Corporations: The Cases of the Electric Companies Enersis and AES Gener

Significance of Chile's Foreign-Owned Corporate Sector

Much of Chile's external debt and short-term financing needs is attributable to foreign-owned companies. The private sector accounts for over 80 percent of the country's external debt, of which about two-thirds corresponds to nonfinancial companies that are mainly or wholly foreign owned. Similarly, foreign-owned companies represent the majority of Chile's sizable short-term gross financing needs. Clearly, any analysis of Chile's external vulnerability needs to consider the financial condition of the foreign-owned corporate sector, as well as how these companies might interact with their foreign parents in times of distress.

Prominent foreign parent companies in Chile include the following (with the local Chilean subsidiary in parentheses): Endesa Spain (Enersis); Telefónica Italia (Entel); Telefónica Spain (CTC); Santander Spain (Banco Santander); BBVA Spain (BBVA Chile); and AES of the United States (AES Gener).

These Chilean subsidiaries have borrowed externally using international bonds or syndicated bank loans in some cases; in others, they have borrowed from their parent companies. These Chilean-resident companies are international not only in their sources of financing, but also because several hold significant investments in other countries.

The Electric Utility Sector: A Tale of Two Companies

Enersis and AES Gener are two Chilean-resident electric companies for which recent developments have provided interesting case studies. Both experienced some difficulties mainly on account of either their own (Enersis) or their parents' (AES Gener) investments in other countries, including Argentina and Brazil.[1] (See Figure.)

The Experience of Enersis

Although official external debt statistics do not provide company-specific information, publicly available information suggests that Enersis is the Chilean-resident company having the largest external debt—over US$9 billion at end-2002, about 14 percent of GDP—and that sizable obligations (around US$2.3 billion) were coming due in 2003 and 2004.

Investments in neighboring countries have hurt Enersis recently. In Argentina, there has been no increase in tariffs for distribution companies in the energy and gas sectors since the devaluation in December 2001. Cash flows from Argentina remain poor. On the back of a 30-year concession agreement, Enersis had made sizable

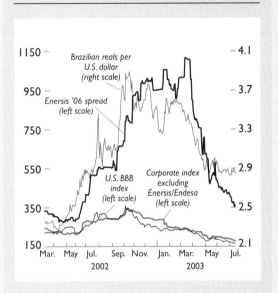

Corporate Bond Spreads and Brazilian Real

Brazilian reals per U.S. dollar (right scale)

Enersis '06 spread (left scale)

U.S. BBB index (left scale)

Corporate index excluding Enersis/Endesa (left scale)

Mar. May Jul. Sep. Nov. Jan. Mar. May Jul.
2002   2003

investments in Argentina, and thus has a vested interest to stay there. In Brazil, tariffs in the energy sector have adjusted in real terms to mitigate potentially large losses to Enersis.

The troubles of Enersis led to concerns about its liquidity, centered around a debt-acceleration clause that would have been triggered in the event of a credit downgrade by Standard & Poor's to subinvestment grade. This concern was signaled by a sharp rise in the spread of its bond maturing in 2006—to over 1,100 basis points.

Investor concern led Endesa Spain to undertake a three-pronged financial restructuring that included generating cash by selling some assets, rescheduling bank loans due in 2003 and 2004, and further capitalization.

- Enersis and its affiliates have sold assets amounting to over US$750 million. These include the sale of their highway and infrastructure affiliates to Spain's OHL for US$273 million, the Río Maipo distribution lines for US$203 million, the Canutillar hydro facility to Belgium's CNPC for US$174 million, and transmission lines to Canada's HKI for US$110 million.

- Enersis and its subsidiary (Endesa Chile) refinanced syndicated loans of US$2.3 billion. The sizable debt service due in 2003 and 2004 (about US$1.4 billion and US$700 million, respectively) is now deferred until 2008. The rollover was negotiated at LIBOR + 350 basis points for Enersis and LIBOR + 300 basis points for Endesa Chile. A key feature in the refinancing deal is the removal of the debt acceleration clause linked to Standard & Poor's rating.

Prepared by Manmohan Singh.

[1]The depreciation of the Chilean peso over the last few years has not greatly affected these companies' operations in Chile because their regulated energy price is linked in part to Chile's exchange rate.

Box 6.1 *(concluded)*

- Endesa Spain, the parent company of Enersis, initiated a capital increase of US$2 billion. The capital increase took the form of a debt-equity swap, prorated and approved by all major creditors. Since Endesa Spain had 65 percent equity in its Chilean subsidiary, the Chilean regulations required approval by all major creditors (including local pension funds) before Endesa increased its ownership in Enersis. Minority shareholders subscribed US$663 million, and Endesa Spain, US$1.22 billion. Bond and equity holders will each have an opportunity to subscribe later in the year (up to the increase's ceiling of US$2 billion).

Investor concerns abated as the financial restructuring advanced. Bond spreads decreased significantly in the spring of 2003, and in July 2003, Endesa Chile was able to issue US$600 million in new long-term external bonds, at spreads close to 450 basis points.

The Enersis case illustrates that corporate vulnerability may be mitigated by the foreign parents of Chilean companies. Chile has been Endesa Spain's gateway into the Latin American energy market, and strategic consideration of long-term potential may have tilted the decision in favor of sustaining Enersis.

The Experience of AES Gener

The case of AES Gener illustrates a "weak parent" situation, with adverse shocks to the parent company having financial repercussions for its Chilean subsidiary. AES's subsidiary in Chile, AES Gener, is rated investment grade locally by S&P-Feller Rate, in light of the subsidiary's strong cash flows (US$180 million annually) and good contracts. However, its foreign parent company, AES, is in difficulty due in part to considerable losses in Argentina and Brazil. Concern about sizable payments due in a few years is reflected in the recent yields of about 16 percent on AES Gener's bonds due in 2005 and 2006.[2]

---

[2]As of May 2003, about 40 percent of AES Gener's bonds were held by Chile's pension funds. These holdings represented less than 1 percent of the pension funds' portfolio.

Unlike Enersis, AES Gener has not received financial support from its foreign parent (which is now rated B+ by Standard & Poor's, with negative outlook). On the contrary, the parent company's financial pinch led it to borrow US$400 million from AES Gener in 2001–02. Subsequently, investors in AES Gener reportedly have been seeking covenants that would limit such flows to the parent company in the future.

Was There "Contagion" from Enersis to Other Chilean Corporations?

Although Enersis could have been perceived as a flagship "Chilean" company, it appears that investors differentiated their assessments of other Chilean companies as a whole from the well-known troubles of Enersis. The level of typical spreads on Chilean corporates has tended to follow rather closely that of the bond index of BBB-rated U.S. companies. When Enersis' spread began to diverge strongly from the U.S. BBB index, starting around mid-2002, spreads for other Chilean companies did not follow along, and in fact generally stayed within 50 basis points of the U.S. BBB spread.

A basic regression analysis (below) also illustrates the explanatory power of the U.S. BBB index in Chilean companies' international bond spreads. Some correlation with Enersis' spread also appears, though with a coefficient one-tenth as large as that on the U.S. BBB index.

$$CHLcorp = 0.66 + 0.78\ USBBB + 0.08\ Enersis + 0.06\ BRZreal$$
$$\quad\quad (2.99)(24.11)\quad\quad (3.33)\quad\quad (0.72)$$

(*t*-statistics in parentheses)

- *CHLcorp* = index of spreads on Chilean corporates (excluding Enersis and Endesa bonds), in logs.
- *US BBB* = index of spreads on the U.S. BBB corporates, in logs.
- *Enersis* = spread of the most relevant Enersis bond, due in 2006, in logs.
- *BRZreal* = value of the Brazilian currency, reals/U.S. dollar, in logs.

---

panies with long-term investment strategies to support their Chilean resident subsidiary in periods of financial stress.

This section first describes the main features of Chile's debt and international investment position. It then presents the medium-term baseline scenario and uses standard sensitivity tests to assess sustainability. Next, it considers gross external financing requirements and develops the sensitivity analysis based on standard shocks as well as a more detailed consideration of rollover rates in the short term. Finally, the section focuses on the implications of the net external position.

Characteristics of the External Position

Chile's total external debt has experienced a steady increase in recent years. From 1997 to 2002, external debt grew by 41 percent in nominal U.S. dollar terms, reaching US$41 billion at the end of 2002 (Figure 6.1). The slowdown in economic activity and depreciation of the Chilean peso also contributed to the rapid increase in the debt-to-GDP ratio, which rose 76 percent during the five-year period. At end-2002, total external debt represented 62 percent of GDP.

Figure 6.1. Evolution of External Debt

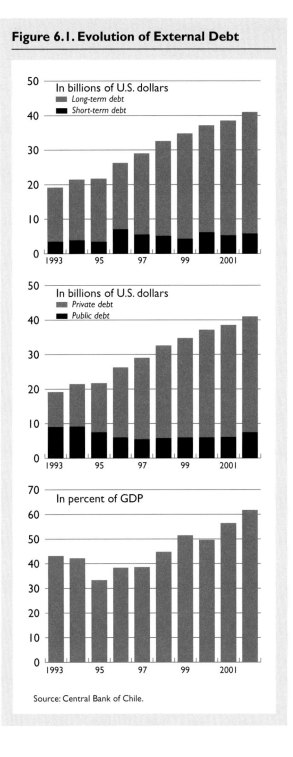

Source: Central Bank of Chile.

trade credits, represented just 6 percent of total debt in 2002 while the duration of the medium-term debt averaged six years. On a residual maturity basis, short-term debt amounted to 18 percent of total debt in 2002.

- Most of the debt is owed to foreign banks (Figure 6.2). About half of long-term debt comes from foreign banks while market bond financing represents a quarter of total long-term debt. (In vulnerability analyses, banks are usually considered more likely to be "supportive" during times of stress than bondholders.)

- Most of the external debt corresponds to the private sector, in particular, foreign-owned companies. The private sector external debt represented 82 percent of the total and foreign-owned firms accounted for 63 percent of that amount (or about 50 percent of total external debt).

- The increase in the external debt was associated with an increase in external asset accumulation by the private sector. Private sector direct investment abroad and portfolio investment tripled from 1997 to 2002, reaching 38 percent of GDP in 2002. Given Chile's supportive investment environment, some foreign multinational firms have used Chile as an investment hub to manage its investments in the region.

- On the other hand, the majority of long-term debt used a floating interest rate, making debt servicing more vulnerable to interest rate fluctuations.

In contrast to the surge in gross external debt, the net external liability position declined in nominal terms during 1997–2002, from US$31 billion to US$28 billion. By 2002, it amounted to 42 percent of GDP, with gross liabilities representing 126 percent of GDP. The stock of direct and equity investment in Chile stood at US$47 billion (56 percent of total liabilities), while direct and equity investment abroad amounted to US$23 billion (Table 6.1).

Compared with other emerging market countries, Chile's international investment position shows a higher degree of financial integration. By end-2001, Chile's total foreign liabilities were the highest among the selected group of emerging market countries. At the same time, Chile had the largest holdings of foreign assets relative to GDP and had among the lowest leverage (ratio of liabilities to assets). Chile had also one of the lowest shares of debt to total liabilities holdings while maintaining a strong external liquidity position. When compared to other Latin American countries, Chile had a high reserve-to-GDP ratio, but was roughly similar to the average of some Eastern European countries and below some East Asian economies (Table 6.2).

Concern about the sharp rise in total external debt, however, should also take into account the following factors:

- Most of this debt is long term (Figure 6.1). Short-term debt on an original maturity basis, excluding

**Figure 6.2. Medium- and Long-Term
External Debt by Type of Creditor, 2002[1]**

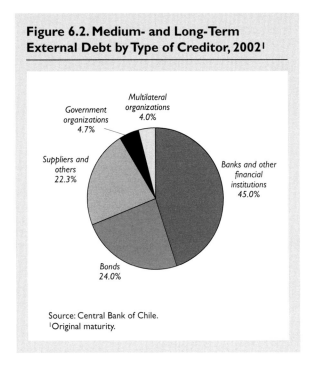

Source: Central Bank of Chile.
[1]Original maturity.

External Debt Sustainability Analysis

Baseline Projections

The baseline scenario prepared by IMF staff assumes a pickup in economic activity over the medium term to close the output gap by 2008. The output growth rate is expected to pick up to 5.5 percent in 2006 before falling back to the growth rate of potential output by 2008. The current account deficit would see a gradual widening from 0.8 percent of GDP in 2002 to 2.5 percent in 2008. Most of the current account deficit would be financed by debt; the baseline has only a modest recovery in net FDI flows reaching about three quarters of the previous decade average level. Nominal external interest rates would increase to 7.0 percent by 2006 and the real exchange rate is projected to be broadly constant over the period. The country risk premium is expected to remain low, at 100–120 basis points.

Under the baseline scenario, total external debt increases from US$41 billion in 2002 to US$57 billion in 2008. The moderate growth in external indebtedness reflects a gradual widening of the current account and some recovery of FDI. The debt-to-GDP ratio is expected to follow a downward path dropping to 54 percent by 2008. The drop in the debt-to-GDP ratio is largely driven by the expected pickup in economic activity.

Sensitivity Analysis

Table 6.3 illustrates the sensitivity of the baseline external debt projection to changes in assumptions. Shocks to real output growth, the current account, the GDP deflator in U.S. dollar terms (a proxy for the real exchange rate), and the level of interest rates during 2003–04 are considered, and the magnitude of each shock is set to be twice the historical standard deviation (calculated over the previous 10 years). Using 10-year historical average values would imply a lower debt-to-GDP path falling to 52 percent at the end of the period.

In all the cases considered, the debt-to-GDP ratio rises considerably during the shock years (2003–2004) before dropping to levels generally higher than the 2002 level. The most significant increase would occur in the extreme and unlikely scenario of a *combination* of two standard deviation negative shocks to the nominal interest rate, real GDP growth, and current account. Similarly, a 20 percent depreciation of the foreign exchange rate would bring external debt to 73 percent of GDP. However, the downside risk of a sharp exchange rate depreciation seems limited, in light of the decline already experienced by the Chilean peso in recent years.[5]

Other Sensitivity Tests

Using information on the international investment position, more specific shocks to income flows from investments abroad are also considered. For instance, a two standard deviation drop of the implicit rate of return of direct and portfolio investments would lead to an increase in the current account deficit of about 0.7 percent of GDP, representing less than half of the current account shock considered above.

The effect of copper price shocks on the current account is also assessed, given that copper exports represent more than one-third of total exports or 10 percent of GDP. Given the high volatility of copper prices, a two standard deviation negative shock to copper prices would drive the average price to a hypothetical 52 cents a pound, or two-thirds of the price assumed under the baseline for 2003. Under this extreme scenario, the direct, static impact on the current account would be on the order of 2 percent of GDP.[6] The effect would have the same order of magnitude as the shock considered in the standard sensitivity test on the current account. The likelihood of such a large negative shock is reduced in light of the broad consensus that copper prices are already in

---

[5]From end-1997 to end-2002, the Chilean peso dropped by 31 percent in real effective terms.

[6]The negative effect on the trade balance would be somewhat larger, but the effect on the current account would be partially offset by reduced profit outflows by foreign-owned mining companies.

Table 6.1. Chile: International Investment Position
(In billions of U.S. dollars)

	1997	1998	1999	2000	2001	2002
Net international position	−31.3	−30.7	−28.7	−29.3	−29.5	−28.0
Assets	35.6	40.9	51.5	52.6	53.1	55.5
Direct investment abroad	5.1	6.7	9.0	11.2	11.9	12.4
Portfolio investment	1.2	4.7	11.4	9.9	10.7	13.0
Equity securities	0.9	3.4	7.7	6.9	7.9	10.5
Debt securities	0.3	1.3	3.7	3.0	2.8	2.5
Other investment	11.1	13.2	16.2	16.4	16.2	14.8
Trade credits	6.3	6.4	7.4	8.5	8.9	8.0
Loans	0.2	0.3	0.5	1.0	1.1	0.7
Currency and deposits	4.6	6.5	8.3	6.9	6.1	6.1
Of which: nonbanking private sector	3.7	5.3	5.8	5.4	4.9	5.0
Reserve assets	18.3	16.3	14.9	15.1	14.4	15.4
Liabilities	67.0	71.6	80.2	81.9	82.6	83.5
Direct investment	34.5	37.6	43.5	45.4	45.1	43.9
Portfolio investment	9.2	8.0	10.6	9.2	10.3	11.1
Equity securities	7.1	5.7	6.5	4.7	3.8	2.9
Debt securities (bonds and notes)	2.1	2.3	4.2	4.5	6.5	8.2
Of which: nonbanking private sector	1.7	1.7	3.1	3.4	4.7	5.3
Other investment	23.3	26.0	26.1	27.3	27.3	28.5
Trade credits	5.6	5.7	5.4	5.6	5.4	5.5
Loans	17.5	20.1	20.7	21.6	21.8	23.0
Of which: nonbanking private sector	13.1	15.8	17.2	18.5	18.2	18.3
Other liabilities	0.2	0.1	0.0	0.1	0.1	0.1

Source: Central Bank of Chile.

Table 6.2. Selected Countries: International Investment Position, 2001
(In percent of GDP)

	Latin America				Eastern Europe			Asia		
	Argentina	Brazil	Chile	Mexico	Czech Republic	Hungary	Poland	Korea	Malaysia	Thailand
Net international position	−33	−52	−43	−37	−12	−56	−32	−15	−18	−43
Assets	49	21	78	17	75	48	26	44	70	47
Direct investment abroad	8	10	17	2	1	4	1	5	10	2
Portfolio investment	9	1	16	1	9	2	1	2	2	1
Other investment	28	3	24	7	38	20	10	13	23	16
Reserve assets	6	7	21	7	26	21	15	24	35	29
Liabilities	83	73	121	54	87	105	58	59	87	90
Direct investment	28	24	66	20	47	43	22	12	24	25
Portfolio investment	28	30	15	22	9	30	10	25	15	15
Other investment	26	19	40	12	30	30	25	22	49	48
Debt to liabilities	65	57	45	63	38	53	57	52	59	62
Liabilities to assets	168	344	156	319	116	217	223	135	125	191
Reserves-to-debt ratio	10	17	38	19	77	37	44	79	68	51

Sources: Central Bank of Chile; and IMF.

Table 6.3. External Debt Sustainability Framework
(In percent of GDP, unless otherwise indicated)

	Actual		Projections					
	2001	2002	2003	2004	2005	2006	2007	2008
	I. Baseline Medium-Term Projections							
External debt	56.5	61.7	59.7	57.2	55.4	54.5	54.0	54.0
Change in external debt	6.8	5.3	–2.1	–2.4	–1.8	–0.9	–0.4	0.0
Identified external debt-creating flows	7.0	7.9	–1.9	–3.8	–4.5	–3.3	–2.7	–2.0
Current account deficit, excluding interest payments	–1.0	–1.6	–1.2	–1.2	–2.1	–1.8	–1.4	–1.0
Deficit in balance of goods and services	–1.7	–2.3	–2.7	–2.3	–2.3	–1.7	–1.2	–0.9
Exports	33.1	33.6	35.7	36.5	36.5	35.9	35.3	34.7
Imports	31.4	31.2	33.0	34.2	34.1	34.2	34.0	33.8
Net non-debt-creating capital inflows (negative)	0.5	5.6	0.5	0.5	–0.8	–0.8	–0.8	–0.7
Net foreign direct investment, equity	4.5	1.7	3.9	2.1	2.0	1.9	1.9	1.7
Net portfolio investment, equity	–5.0	–7.3	–4.3	–2.6	–1.2	–1.1	–1.0	–1.0
Automatic debt dynamics[1]	7.5	3.9	–1.2	–3.1	–1.7	–0.8	–0.5	–0.3
Contribution from nominal interest rate	2.5	2.3	1.6	1.9	3.2	3.6	3.5	3.5
Contribution from real GDP growth	–1.5	–1.2	–1.8	–2.4	–2.7	–2.8	–2.5	–2.4
Contribution from price and exchange rate changes[2]	6.5	2.8	–1.0	–2.6	–2.1	–1.5	–1.5	–1.4
Residual, including change in gross foreign assets	–0.2	–2.6	–0.2	1.4	2.7	2.4	2.2	2.0
External debt-to-exports ratio (in percent)	170.7	183.9	167.2	157.0	151.9	151.6	153.1	155.6
Gross external financing need (in billions of U.S. dollars)[3]	11.6	11.6	11.2	9.8	11.6	12.5	12.2	13.0
In percent of GDP	17.0	17.5	16.1	12.9	14.0	13.9	12.5	12.4
Key macroeconomic and external assumptions								
Real GDP growth (in percent)	2.8	2.2	3.1	4.4	5.2	5.5	5.0	4.8
Exchange rate appreciation (U.S. dollar value of local currency, change in percent)	–15.0	–7.8	–2.9	1.3	0.0	0.0	0.0	0.0
GDP deflator in U.S. dollars (change in percent)	–11.5	–4.7	1.7	4.6	3.8	2.9	2.8	2.7
Nominal external interest rate (in percent)	4.7	4.0	2.8	3.5	6.0	7.0	7.0	7.0
Growth of exports (U.S. dollar terms, in percent)	–3.1	–1.2	11.4	11.6	9.2	6.9	6.0	5.9
Growth of imports (U.S. dollar terms, in percent)	–1.8	–3.2	10.8	13.0	9.0	8.8	7.4	6.9
	II. Stress Tests for External Debt Ratio							
Real GDP growth, nominal interest rate, U.S. dollar deflator, noninterest current account, and nondebt inflows at historical average in 2003–08		61.7	58.1	56.0	55.3	54.3	53.2	51.8
Nominal interest rate is at historical average plus two standard deviations in 2003 and 2004		61.7	62.1	61.4	59.4	58.4	58.0	57.9
Real GDP growth is at historical average minus two standard deviations in 2003 and 2004		61.7	62.7	64.1	62.3	61.4	61.1	61.2
Change in U.S. dollar GDP deflator is at historical average minus two standard deviations in 2003 and 2004		61.7	66.4	73.2	71.4	70.6	70.4	70.7
Noninterest current account is at historical average minus two standard deviations in 2003 and 2004		61.7	65.5	68.7	66.5	65.4	64.9	64.8
Combination of shocks using one standard deviation		61.7	72.5	86.9	84.1	82.7	82.1	82.0
One-time 20 percent nominal depreciation in 2003		61.7	72.7	70.0	68.2	67.4	67.2	67.3

Historical statistics for key variables (past 10 years)	Historical Average	Standard Deviation	Average 2002–07
Current account deficit, excluding interest payments	0.3	2.1	–1.4
Net non-debt-creating capital inflows	1.7	3.2	0.4
Nominal external interest rate (in percent)	5.3	0.8	5.6
Real GDP growth (in percent)	5.6	3.8	4.7
GDP deflator in U.S. dollars (change in percent)	1.6	9.8	3.1

Sources: Central Bank of Chile; and IMF staff calculations.

[1]Derived as $[r – g – \rho(1 + g) + \varepsilon\alpha(1 + r)]/(1 + g + \rho + g\rho)$ times previous period debt stock, where r = nominal effective interest rate on external debt; ρ = change in domestic GDP deflator in U.S. dollar terms, g = real GDP growth rate, ε = nominal appreciation (increase in dollar value of domestic currency), and α = share of domestic-currency-denominated debt in total external debt.

[2]The contribution from price and exchange rate changes is defined as $[–\rho(1 + g) + \varepsilon\alpha(1 + g + \rho + g\rho)]$ times previous period debt stock. ρ increases with an appreciating domestic currency (e > 0) and rising inflation (based on GDP deflator).

[3]Defined as current account deficit, plus amortization on medium- and long-term debt, plus short-term debt at end of previous period.

Table 6.4. Gross External Financing Requirement
(In billions of U.S. dollars, unless otherwise indicated)

	Actual				Projections			
	1999	2000	2001	2002	2003	2004	2005	2006
Gross external financing need in billions of U.S. dollars[1]	8.4	8.9	11.6	11.6	11.2	9.8	11.6	12.5
In percent of GDP	11.5	11.9	17.0	17.5	16.1	12.9	14.0	13.9
Noninterest current account deficit	−1.8	−1.3	−0.7	−1.1	−0.8	−0.9	−1.7	−1.6
Debt and debt service falling due	10.2	10.2	12.3	12.7	12.0	10.7	13.4	14.1
Amortizations	3.4	3.8	4.2	5.8	5.0	3.4	4.9	5.0
Of which: debt prepayments	0.8	1.1	1.7	1.6	0.0	0.0	0.0	0.0
Debt service	1.7	2.1	1.9	1.6	1.1	1.5	2.6	3.2
Short-term debt	5.1	4.3	6.2	5.3	5.8	5.8	5.8	5.8
Gross external financing need in billions of U.S. dollars[2]								
Real GDP growth, nominal interest rate, dollar deflator, noninterest current account, and non-debt inflows are at historical average in 2003–07					13.5	12.0	13.7	14.1
Nominal interest rate is at historical average plus two standard deviations in 2003 and 2004					13.0	11.7	12.6	13.5
Real GDP growth is at historical average minus two standard deviations in 2003 and 2004					11.2	9.9	11.9	12.8
Change in U.S. dollar GDP deflator is at historical average minus two standard deviations in 2003 and 2004					11.3	10.0	12.1	13.1
Noninterest current account is at historical average minus two standard deviations in 2003 and 2004					15.7	15.6	14.3	15.3
Combination of shocks using one standard deviation					15.5	14.7	14.0	15.0
One time 20 percent nominal depreciation in 2003					11.3	10.0	12.1	13.0
Gross external financing need in percent of GDP[2]								
Real GDP growth, nominal interest rate, U.S. dollar deflator, noninterest current account and nondebt inflows at historical average in 2003–08					18.8	15.3	16.2	15.4
Nominal interest rate is at historical average plus two standard deviations in 2003 and 2004					18.7	15.4	15.2	15.0
Real GDP growth is at historical average minus two standard deviations in 2003 and 2004					16.9	14.5	16.0	15.8
Change in U.S. dollar GDP deflator is at historical average minus two standard deviations in 2003 and 2004					18.0	16.7	18.5	18.4
Noninterest current account is at historical average minus two standard deviations in 2003 and 2004					22.6	20.6	17.2	17.0
Combination of shocks using one standard deviation					24.7	24.9	21.7	21.5
One-time 20 percent nominal depreciation in 2003					19.8	15.9	17.6	17.5

Sources: Central Bank of Chile; and IMF staff calculations.

[1]Defined as noninterest current account deficit, plus interest and amortization on medium- and long-term debt, plus short-term debt at end of previous period.

[2]Gross external financing under the stress-test scenarios is derived by assuming the same ratio of short-term to total debt as in the baseline scenario and the same average maturity on medium- and long-term debt. Interest expenditures are derived by applying the respective interest rate to the previous period's debt stock under each alternative scenario.

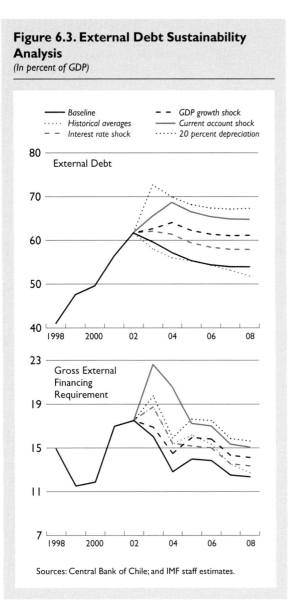

Figure 6.3. External Debt Sustainability Analysis
(In percent of GDP)

Sources: Central Bank of Chile; and IMF staff estimates.

2002. The amortization payments of medium- and long-term debt represent the bulk of financing requirements. Most of the recent increase in amortization payments follows from the rise of external borrowing in the early and mid-1990s as it comes due (see Table 6.4 above). In addition, actual amortization exceeded scheduled amortization in 2001 and 2002, as firms chose to prepay external debt and shift toward domestic financing.

Under the baseline, total annual gross external financing requirements are expected to decline from a high of 17.5 percent as a share of GDP in 2002 to 14 percent in 2006. The drop is largely driven by the expected surplus in noninterest current account throughout the projection period and the pickup in economic growth. Also, medium- and long-term debt amortization payments are not expected to rise beyond the 2002 level, as important payments coming due in 2003 to 2004 have been recently rescheduled.[8] The baseline assumes that short-term debt remains constant in nominal terms. We assume that about two-thirds of the external debt has floating interest rates, broadly consistent with past experience.

Sensitivity Analysis Test

The sensitivity tests underscore again the responsiveness of external requirements to changes in assumptions (Table 6.4 and Figure 6.3). In particular, the external requirement is most sensitive to a shock in the current account that would bring it to over 22 percent of GDP. All other shocks would keep the external financing needs below 19 percent of GDP. None of the shocks considered would bring the total financing requirements above official international reserves (now almost 25 percent of GDP). Moreover, private sector liquid foreign asset holdings (considering only currency and deposits) amounted in 2002 to 8 percent of GDP, representing more than two-thirds of the private sector's short-term external debt on a residual maturity basis.

Net External Position

Chile's foreign asset position is a source of strength. We consider three aspects of Chile's international investment position (IIP) that would dampen the effects of the shocks considered in the previous sections. First, we underscore the role of Chile's large FDI liabilities in providing external support in periods of stress. Second, we note the

the low end of the cycle, below their medium- or long-run levels. Also, such a price would be considerably below the cost floor of many of the world's copper mines, and below the real prices at which mines began to shut down during the late 1990s.[7]

Gross External Financing Requirements

Total gross external financing requirements have risen in recent years to reach 17.5 percent of GDP in

---

[7]See IMF (2002).

[8]Enersis recently agreed with foreign banks to reschedule its loan commitment worth US$2 billion coming due in 2003 and 2004 beyond 2008 (Box 6.1).

Table 6.5. External Balance Sheet Indicators
(In percent)

	1997	1998	1999	2000	2001	2002
Leverage indicators						
Liabilities to assets	188	175	156	156	156	150
Debt to assets	71	69	59	60	64	66
Net liabilities to GDP	38	39	39	39	43	42
Net debt to GDP	17	17	14	17	22	29
Liquidity indicators[1]						
Liquid assets to total assets	64	56	45	42	39	39
Liquid assets to non-FDI liabilities	70	67	63	60	55	54
Reserves to GDP	22	21	20	20	21	23
Private sector liquid assets to GDP	6	8	11	9	9	9

Sources: Central Bank of Chile; and IMF staff estimates.
[1]Liquid assets include only international reserves and currency and deposits abroad.

solid liquid asset position, including the significant foreign liquid assets held by the private sector. Third, we follow a balance sheet approach to show the counterbalancing effect of shocks on the aggregate net asset position of the country.

The country's large FDI liabilities are a source of external support in periods of stress. As shown in Table 6.2, the relative size of foreign direct investment in Chile stands out when compared to other emerging market economies. The necessary counterpart of these investments is the large share of direct investment income outflows in the external current account. This component has important implications on how the current account adjusts to shocks affecting domestic activity.

Sensitivity analysis on the implicit rate of return on foreign investment shows that a one standard deviation negative shock would lead to a GDP improvement of 2 percent in the noninterest current account. Given the likely high correlation between changes in the output level and implicit rates of return, a sharp drop in output growth would bring a sharp adjustment in the current account driven by lower investment income outflows, everything else constant.

Chile's liquid assets, of both the public and private sectors, appear to rule out reasonable liquidity risks (Table 6.5). At end-2002, total liquid external assets—even on a narrow definition—amounted to US$21 billion (32 percent of GDP), accounted for more than half of total external gross debt, and covered about 2.6 times gross external financing requirements. Liquid holdings by the private sector, considering a narrow definition that includes only foreign deposit and currency holdings, amounted to US$5 billion at end-2002.

The picture is only more favorable if one considers short-term trade credits owed to Chilean firms. At end-2002 these amounted to 12 percent of GDP. Empirical evidence shows that these types of credits have a low probability of default, thus providing further support to the strength of Chile's aggregate balance sheet.[9]

The balance sheet effect of a foreign exchange depreciation shock has no negative effect on the net asset position as a share of GDP. If we assume that FDI liabilities are denominated in local currency, then the reduction on FDI liabilities from the exchange rate depreciation would more than compensate for the drop in the U.S. dollar value of GDP. For example, a 20 percent depreciation of the peso would lower the ratio of net liabilities to GDP from 42 percent to 32 percent, and would reduce the ratio of liabilities to assets from 150 percent to 129 percent.

References

International Monetary Fund, 2000, "Assessing External Vulnerability: The Case of Chile," in *Chile—Selected Issues*, IMF Staff Country Report No. 00/104 (Washington: International Monetary Fund).

[9]For recent studies, see Nilsen (2002) and Ng, Kiholm Smith, and Smith (1999).

———, 2002, "Forecasting Copper Prices in the Chilean Context," in *Chile—Selected Issues*, IMF Country Report No. 02/163 (Washington: International Monetary Fund).

Ng, C.K., J. Kiholm Smith, and R. Smith, 1999, "Evidence on the Determinants of Credit Terms Used in Interfirm Trade," *Journal of Finance*, Vol. 54, No. 3 (June), pp. 1109–29.

Nilsen, J., 2002, "Trade Credit and the Bank Lending Channel," *Journal of Money, Credit and Banking*, Vol. 34, No. 1 (February), pp. 226–53.

VII   Public Sector Finances: Balance Sheets, Financing Needs, and Sustainability

Steven Phillips

This section examines the financial position of the Chilean public sector. The focus is on analysis of balance sheet information, taking account of financial assets as well as liabilities, and of the structure of balance sheets, in terms of foreign exchange position and liquidity. The analysis is facilitated by recent enhancements of the available information, especially by the Public Debt Report issued for the first time in late 2002.[1]

The analysis begins at the central government level, where account is taken of the government's structural balance target and is then broadened to consider other parts of the public sector: in turn the central bank and the public enterprises. Significantly, subnational governments in Chile are subject to strict budget constraints (see Section III) and indeed have no financial debt. Accordingly they are not analyzed here.

The central government has been in the past, and will likely continue to be, the key to movements in Chile's total public debt. Still, attention is due also to the central bank accounts, because the bank's total debt is significant (as are its assets), and because much of the central government's debt is owed to the central bank. For some purposes, it is useful to analyze the consolidated central government/central bank position.

The assessment of the public sector finances is favorable. Since risky balance sheet structures have been avoided, exposure to currency and interest rate risks is limited. Taking account of the government's structural balance target, it is difficult to see debt sustainability problems emerging, as long as this target (or other restrained fiscal policy) is implemented. The central bank's balance sheet is also examined, noting its considerable strengths in terms of foreign exchange and liquidity positions, but also its tendency to imply an operating deficit. Though the bank's deficit has been fairly stable and has not interfered with its monetary policy objectives, its situation is not ideal, and some steps, including a capital injection from the government, that could be

taken are noted. Less complex is the situation of the public enterprises: their aggregate position appears sound, in light of their overall profitability and limited indebtedness. On the whole, the public enterprise sector is an asset rather than a drain on government finances.

Central Government Finances

Significant aspects of the central government's balance sheet are the following:

- Substantial financial assets, about 5 percent of GDP in 2002, mostly claims on the private sector. (In recent years, the drawdown of such assets has played an important role, financing about half of the government's deficit.)

- Gross debt is relatively low, about 16 percent of GDP in 2002.

- Debt to the domestic private sector is zero.

- Almost two-thirds of the government's gross debt is owed to the central bank. This old debt was issued in 1983 to compensate for the balance sheet effect of a financial sector bailout (Section II); it is mostly denominated in U.S. dollars.

- The remainder is external debt, also mainly denominated in U.S. dollars. More than half of this debt consists of medium- or long-term sovereign bonds, all issued within the last several years. Most other external debt is owed to international institutions.

- The average interest rate is quite low. For example, the ratio of interest payments to government debt was only about 2 percent in 2002 (and about 4 percent over the previous 10 years).

Financing Needs

Gross financing needs can be expected to remain moderate:

- The government does not face a steep amortization schedule, as the average maturity of its debt

---

[1]Ministry of Finance (2002).

is evidently rather long. Thus from an existing debt stock of 16 percent of GDP at end-2002, amortization will be only 1 to 1½ percent of GDP annually during 2003–06 (and will rise only moderately thereafter).[2]

- The fiscal deficit is modest, not more than 1 percent of GDP for 2003, and is expected to decline in the next few years.

- A further consideration is that the government has some room to further reduce its financial assets.

Exposure to Currency Depreciation

Currency depreciation does not pose a major risk to the public finances. While most of the government's financial assets now are denominated in domestic currency, nearly all of its debt is denominated in U.S. dollars. Considering only these two quantities, the government's net foreign exchange position would appear to have been about –14 percent of GDP at end-2002. Taking a broader view, however, the picture improves:

- Account needs also to be taken of the stream of foreign currency earnings the government receives, mainly from its ownership of the copper company CODELCO. Though this income varies with world copper prices, in most years, the government's primary balance on foreign-denominated flows is positive.

- Most of the government's U.S. dollar debt—and thus most of its dollar-denominated interest bill also—is owed to the central bank. In turn, the central bank has a substantial positive net foreign exchange position (as discussed in the next section, about +23 percent of GDP at end-2002).

Exposure to Interest Rate Fluctuations

As a consequence of the structure of its debt, the government has little near-term exposure to interest rate shocks. In fact, the government is nearly unaffected by domestic interest rate fluctuations. The avoidance of short-term external debt means there is also little near-term exposure to changes in the risk premium international investors apply to Chilean sovereign debt.

The government's interest rate exposure is largely confined to fluctuations in world interest rates. This

is because interest on the government's old debt to the central bank is tied to the London interbank offered rate.

Sustainability of Central Government Debt

Debt sustainability analysis for Chile must take into account the government's commitment to an ongoing target for its structural balance (see Section II). As long as this practice is maintained, it is difficult to see problems of debt sustainability emerging, in light of two basic considerations:

- As long as the structural balance rule is followed, *debt dynamics are unaffected by a rise in interest rates on government debt:* since the target refers to the entire government balance, any increase in the interest bill would have to be offset by a policy reaction to tighten the government's primary balance.

- *Most important to debt sustainability is the level chosen for the targeted structural balance: a surplus of 1 percent of GDP.* It is true that this figure does not take account of the central bank's deficit (discussed below), and that if a broader view of the public sector were taken, the effective level of the target would not be quite as strong; however, it still would not represent a deficit. Thus the government debt/GDP ratio could well be expected to decline over time even if economic growth were zero.

There is one significant complication to this picture: the fiscal target refers to the government's *structural, not actual,* balance. Whereas the target refers to a cyclically adjusted balance, the evolution of government debt of course depends on the actual balance. Therefore, the structural balance rule does not alone determine the exact path of public debt, and further analysis is needed.

Under the rule holding the structural balance constant, the path of public debt depends not only on the chosen level of the fiscal target, but also on the estimated cyclical adjustments. More precisely, given Chile's fiscal rule, projecting government debt requires projecting not only *actual* output and copper export prices, but also (the estimates of) *potential* GDP and the *reference* copper export price, which will together determine how far the actual government balance deviates from the level of the structural balance target.

Table 7.1 illustrates how the central government gross debt ratio would evolve under various combinations of actual and (estimated) potential output paths. The starting point is the baseline scenario in which the output gap, currently estimated about 5 percent, would close gradually over the medium

---

[2]Most of the amortization due relates to the government's old debt to the central bank. There is no possibility of rolling over this debt, or refinancing it with fresh funds from the central bank, since Chile's constitution (see Section III) prohibits the central bank from financing the government.

Table 7.1. Sensitivity of Government Debt Projections Under the Structural Balance Rule

	2002	2003	2004	2005	2006	2007	2008
Structural balance (percent of GDP)		0.8	1.0	1.0	1.0	1.0	1.0
Baseline scenario							
GDP growth, actual (percent)		3.3	4.5	5.2	5.5	5.0	4.8
GDP growth, potential (percent)		3.7	3.7	3.8	4.0	4.2	4.5
Output gap (deviation from potential, percent)		–4.8	–4.0	–2.7	–1.2	–0.4	–0.1
Actual balance (percent of GDP)		–0.8	–0.1	0.4	0.7	0.8	0.9
Government gross debt (percent of GDP)	15.9	15.6	14.5	13.0	11.3	9.6	8.0
Alternative scenarios							
1. Baseline, *except:* higher estimate of potential output							
GDP growth, actual (percent)		3.3	4.5	5.2	5.5	5.0	4.8
GDP growth, potential (percent)		3.7	6.4	7.0	5.5	5.0	4.8
Output gap (deviation from potential, percent)		–4.8	–6.5	–8.0	–8.0	–8.0	–8.0
Actual balance (percent of GDP)		–0.6	–0.6	–0.7	–0.7	–0.7	–0.6
Government gross debt (percent of GDP)	15.9	15.4	14.8	14.3	13.9	13.5	13.2
2. Baseline, *except:* low actual growth, with some downward revision to estimate of potential growth							
GDP growth, actual (percent)		3.3	2.0	2.0	2.0	2.0	2.0
GDP growth, potential (percent)		3.7	3.7	3.8	2.2	2.0	2.0
Output gap (deviation from potential, percent)		–4.8	–6.3	–7.9	–8.0	–8.0	–8.0
Actual balance (percent of GDP)		–0.6	–0.6	–0.7	–0.7	–0.7	–0.7
Government gross debt (percent of GDP)	15.9	15.4	15.1	15.0	15.0	15.0	14.9
3. Baseline, *except:* low actual growth, with no downward revision to potential output estimate							
GDP growth, actual (percent)		3.3	2.0	2.0	2.0	2.0	2.0
GDP growth, potential (percent)		3.7	3.7	3.8	4.0	4.2	4.5
Output gap (deviation from potential, percent)		–4.8	–6.3	–7.9	–9.6	–11.5	–13.5
Actual balance (percent of GDP)		–0.6	–0.6	–0.7	–1.0	–1.4	–1.7
Government gross debt (percent of GDP)	15.9	15.4	15.1	15.0	15.3	15.9	17.0

Source: IMF staff estimates and projections.

term. In that scenario, the debt/GDP ratio would decline from 16 percent to 8 percent of GDP by 2008. Several alternative scenarios demonstrate that some rather unlikely assumptions would be needed to generate a rising debt/GDP ratio:

- In the first scenario, actual growth follows the baseline scenario, but a burst of optimism about potential output takes the estimated output gap up to 8 percent. The actual deficit is therefore larger than in the baseline scenario, but the government debt ratio still declines somewhat.

- In the second scenario, the output gap is again 8 percent, but this time with actual growth held to just 2 percent and combined with a somewhat less optimistic estimate of potential output. Again, the debt ratio fails to increase.

- Finally, the third scenario combines a low actual growth rate with an assumption that estimated

potential output is no less than in the baseline scenario. The estimated output gap rises to an implausible 14 percent, and this time the debt ratio does begin to rise, after a few years.

Again, these examples are not intended to represent plausible scenarios, only to illustrate the degree of sensitivity of debt dynamics under the structural balance rule.

More practically, under this fiscal rule, the estimate of the output gap is updated regularly. This updating is done with the help of an expert panel, providing the opportunity to lower the estimate of potential output in the event that actual growth turns out less than expected. Moreover, this estimation is performed within a methodological framework (the Hodrick-Prescott filter) that penalizes large gaps between actual and potential output estimates. In this light, the above examples are seen to be artificial, as it is unlikely that an output gap estimate as high as

8 percent would be sustained year after year. Broadly similar considerations apply to the other adjustment used in the structural balance, which relates to the copper export price gap.[3]

Thus while uncertainty about the size and duration of (estimated) cyclical adjustments used in the structural balance rule is relevant for debt projections, plausible degrees of error (or "optimism") on potential output along the way would not lead to unstable debt dynamics.[4]

Central Bank Finances

The balance sheet of the Central Bank of Chile has these essential features:

- Large size. Assets and liabilities together total about 70 percent of GDP. Assets are dominated by international reserves, along with some (old) central government debt. Liabilities are dominated by domestic debt issues.[5]

- Strong liquidity position. While assets are dominated by liquid foreign assets, liabilities are mostly medium-term paper. Importantly, the bank has avoided any issuance of short-term debt indexed to the exchange rate; it also has avoided interest rate indexation.

- A significant currency mismatch, the bank being long in dollars. Assets that are exchange rate–linked far exceed exchange rate–linked liabilities (Table 7.2). At end-2002, the net foreign exchange position was +23 percent of GDP.

Assessment of Risks

The structure of the bank's balance sheet is not problematic. As noted, the bank's balance sheet is strong in terms of liquidity. As for exchange rate exposure, strictly speaking, the bank's currency mismatch is a source of risk: for example, a 10 percent appreciation (depreciation) of the peso rate produces a valuation loss (gain) in excess of 2 percent of GDP. However, this exposure is in the right direction to be considered a form of insurance.[6] Thus if "bad times"

for the Chilean economy cause the currency to depreciate, there will be associated gains for the central bank, lowering net debt of the public sector as a whole and so helping to support confidence. On the other hand, losses from currency appreciation would tend to be associated with favorable circumstances (e.g., terms of trade improvement), times in which confidence would be improving.

The central bank's currency mismatch has declined in recent years, and it may be reduced further. Since 1997, the significant issuance of U.S. dollar–indexed debt has reduced the exposure of the central bank, and the public sector more broadly, to appreciation of the domestic currency. Looking forward, it is possible that the denomination of the government debt owed to the central bank will be switched from dollars to pesos.[7] This would distribute exposure to peso appreciation more evenly within the public sector.

The Central Bank Deficit: Implications and Outlook

The central bank's balance on operations has tended to be negative. Rather than from current central bank policies, these losses arise from: (1) the government exercising its option to capitalize interest on its old debt to the central bank; and (2) the inherited structure of the balance sheet, related to the support to banks in the 1980s and to sterilized exchange market intervention during part of the 1990s.[8] In recent years, the IMF staff's measure of the central bank deficit has been close to 1 percent of GDP on a cash basis, and about 0.5 percent of GDP on an accrual basis.[9]

Though the central bank's deficit is moderate in size and seems to be stable, it is not to be ignored. The Chilean government explicitly recognized the significance of the central bank's deficit when it chose to set the target for the central government balance at a small surplus. A further consideration is the potential link between a central bank's financial strength and its effectiveness.[10] There has been no sign that the Chilean central bank's deficit has interfered with its effective independence, but it is possible that public perceptions of the bank's indepen-

---

[3]For an analysis of sustainability issues in light of uncertainty over copper export prices, also with generally favorable conclusions, see (IMF, 2002a), Chapter III.

[4]A key factor limiting the sensitivity of debt projections in this context is the relatively small adjustment allowed under the structural balance rule for a given output gap (see Section II).

[5]Credit to banks and monetary liabilities are relatively small components of the balance sheet.

[6]Whether this degree of insurance is optimal to Chile's circumstances is a technically challenging question beyond the scope of this section.

[7]Such a move has already been approved by the congress; what remains is for the government and central bank to agree on technical details.

[8]See Appendix III of the staff report for the 2002 Article IV consultation for a fuller discussion of the bank's flow losses and their origin (IMF, 2002b).

[9]This measure does not include capital gains/losses arising from currency fluctuations. In recent years, the bank has experienced large capital gains as a consequence of the peso's depreciation against the U.S. dollar.

[10]See, for example, Stella (2002).

Table 7.2. Components of Central Bank Net Debt, 2002
(In percent of GDP)

Assets		Liabilities	
Foreign-denominated		Foreign-denominated (or indexed)	
International reserves	23.9	Foreign liabilities	0.0
Government debt	9.1	Government deposits	0.7
		U.S. dollar–indexed paper	9.3
Peso-denominated		Peso-denominated	
Government debt	0.7	Government deposits	0.3
		Peso paper	21.5
		Of which: inflation-indexed	9.3

Source: Central Bank of Chile.

dence could be diminished by the existence of a deficit (especially if the deficit were to begin to grow, though this is not expected). At the least, the bank's deficit complicates understanding of the public sector's financial position.

Steps could be taken to clarify the financial relationship between the government and central bank. One step would be for the government to pay full accrued interest on its debt to the central bank (i.e., declining to utilize its option to capitalize some of this interest). Going further, the government could consider a more comprehensive solution, ending the bank's deficit entirely by an appropriately sized recapitalization. Such a move could for example take the form of a transfer of government bonds to the bank; alternatively, it might be possible to transfer to the government responsibility for a part of the domestic debt now on the bank's balance sheet.

The Chilean authorities are currently engaged in technical work to better understand the central bank deficit. Despite its apparent stability in recent years, the bank's balance is subject to change from a number of factors, though these sometimes offset one another. The Chilean authorities aim to estimate the bank's *underlying* deficit—a difficult exercise, taking into account, inter alia, cycles in interest rates (including variations in term structure) and exchange rates. Although this section cannot anticipate the results of that exercise, two qualitative points on the outlook for the bank's deficit can be noted. One is that *the bank's net flows are likely to improve in the period ahead,* especially as debt issued some years ago at much higher interest rates comes due and is replaced with cheaper debt. Another is simply to observe, in light of the bank's sizable currency mismatch, that projections of the central bank balance will be sensitive to exchange rate assumptions.

Finances of the Public Enterprise Sector

Significant aspects of the public enterprise sector's balance sheet are the following:

- Net debt of about 6 percent of GDP: gross debt being about 6½ percent of GDP, and financial assets about ½ percent of GDP, at end-2002.

- Gross debt is mainly—about three-fourths—external. Domestic debt remains small, still less than 2 percent of GDP, though in recent years a few enterprises, including CODELCO and the Metro, have issued bonds locally.

- The average interest rate is low: for example, the ratio of interest payments to gross debt was only 3.5 percent in 2002. (For CODELCO, the company that accounts for the largest share of public enterprise debt, interest payments were only 2 percent of current income in 2002, a year not only of low interest rates but also relatively weak copper prices.)

- Maturity of debt: about three-quarters of the public enterprise sector's debt to the private sector is long term.[11]

In terms of flows, the public enterprise sector has been performing favorably in recent years. In particular, its balance on current account—after sending taxes and profits to the central government—has been fairly steady, at around 1 percent of GDP. Its overall balance has been in modest deficit, reflecting

---

[11]An annual amortization schedule for public enterprise sector debt is not available. However, the Public Debt Report gives the breakdown between short-term and all other debt, as noted here.

capital expenditure usually between 1 and 2 percent of GDP. (The majority of such capital expenditure has been by CODELCO, which is now well into a multiyear plan to expand its capacity.)

Interpretation

Under current circumstances, the public enterprise sector is not critical to the analysis of possible debt sustainability problems of the Chilean public sector. Partly this is because this sector represents a minor share (less than 15 percent) of total public debt. More fundamentally, the public enterprise sector seems to be run mainly on commercial principles and in any case is on the whole profitable. At the same time, it is advisable to continue to monitor the condition of the public enterprise sector, as it is large enough to be of macroeconomic significance, and to be alert to any change in its financial position.

Transparency and analysis of the public enterprise sector are set to take a step forward. The authorities are now developing a new set of statistics to follow the new standard set by the IMF's 2001 *Government Finance Statistics*, with its accrual basis and emphasis on capturing changes in net worth. In particular, the new set of statistics will include information on the value of the fixed assets of this sector, and on capital consumption flows (depreciation).

References

International Monetary Fund, 2002a, "Chile: Selected Issues," IMF Country Report No. 02/163 (Washington: International Monetary Fund).

———, 2002b, "Chile: 2002 Article IV Consultation—Staff Report; Staff Statement; Public Information Notice on the Executive Board Discussion; and Statement by the Executive Director for Chile," IMF Country Report No. 02/155 (Washington: International Monetary Fund).

Ministry of Finance, 2002, *Estadísticas de la Deuda Pública*, October. Available via the Internet at http://www.minhda.cl/castellano/inicio.html.

Stella, P., 2002, "Central Bank Financial Strength, Transparency, and Policy Credibility," IMF Working Paper No. 02/137 (Washington: International Monetary Fund).

VIII   Export Specialization and Economic Growth

Mauricio Villafuerte

Claims in the recent economic literature that natural resource–based exports have a negative impact on long-term economic growth have raised some concerns about the structure and evolution of Chile's exports.[1] Exports in Chile have been very dynamic in recent decades but have decelerated somewhat in recent years, while the structure of exports continues to be dominated by natural resources. This section asks whether the structure of Chilean exports has worked in favor of or against a sustained economic growth and looks into how the country could continue to improve its current "export model." It argues that

- Chile has not been subject to the "curse" of natural resources endowment, because it has avoided the main factors that the economic literature identifies as reasons for a negative impact of natural resource–based exports on economic growth.

- Chile has developed several export industries based on its natural resource endowments, with important spillovers to economic activity, a combination of static comparative advantages with knowledge and innovation.

- To increase overall productivity and the diversification of Chilean exports, government policies should concentrate on improving education levels.

- The government should continue to deepen its trade liberalization efforts, with the current "open regionalism" strategy being an adequate mechanism to increase the market access of Chilean exports.

- The recent weak export growth can be traced to the difficult external environment.

This section first examines the reasons why natural resources in Chile have not been detrimental to growth, the factors behind the recent evolution of exports, and the link between exports and growth in Chile. It concludes by discussing potential trade specialization patterns through the creation of new comparative advantages.

Exports of Natural Resources and Growth in Chile

Can natural resource–based exports help sustain economic growth in Chile? This question is motivated by (1) an economic literature that reports a negative impact of natural resource abundance on economic growth rates (due in part to limited spillovers from natural resource–based export products); and (2) the recent deceleration of export growth in Chile. This section presents arguments that contrast these facts with the Chilean experience.

The "Curse" of Natural Resources

The idea that natural resource endowment could work against economic development is not a new one, but has received increased attention in recent years in light of cross-country empirical research. In particular, Sachs and Warner (1995) found a negative relationship between natural resource exports and growth rates of economic activity, though their findings are not uncontroversial.[2]

The explanations offered by the theoretical literature that postulates a negative impact of natural resource exports on growth can be broadly grouped as follows:

- Political economy dynamics by which interest groups fight to capture the rents from natural resources. These "voracity effects" (which are particularly acute in the case of government-con-

---

[1]For example, Sachs and Warner (1995), Auty (1990), and Gelb and others (1988).

[2]Lederman and Maloney (2002) argue that the findings of Sachs and Warner are probably due to unaccounted for country-specific effects and do not hold when applied to other periods of time or after dealing with endogeneity issues. By contrast, they emphasize the negative correlation between export concentration and growth.

trolled natural resources) reveal themselves in "rent-seeking" activities, inefficient taxation,[3] and distortionary economic policies in general, and lead to a bad allocation of resources and, hence, lower economic growth.

• Explanations focused on the productive structure of the economy, stressing the inability of natural resource exports to generate key linkages among activities generating spillovers on aggregate output. The development literature of the 1940s and 1950s made the case against resource-based growth on (1) the premise of a secular decline in world prices of primary exports relative to manufactures; (2) poor potential for productivity growth of natural resource sectors; and (3) small "forward and backward linkages" from primary exports to the rest of the economy.[4]

• Dutch Disease. A boom in natural resource exports leads to an appreciation of the real exchange rate that in turn produces a reallocation of factors of production away from other tradables. In the long run, this process would increase the dependence on natural resource exports and, hence, limit the sources of economic growth.[5]

The Chilean Case

Chile has not been subject to the factors identified by the literature as a "curse" of natural resources, namely (1) the exports of natural resources have not crowded out other promising sectors; (2) the relative importance of nonprocessed natural resource exports has consistently fallen; (3) productivity in natural resource–based sectors has increased in the last 25 years; and (4) new export products have been developed, partly on the basis of technological spillovers from natural resource exports (as will be shown below).

Indeed, the recent copper mining boom (in the early and mid-1990s) did not have a negative impact on other export sectors. According to several studies, it produced a very limited crowding out of investments from other sectors and, in fact, had an overall positive impact on the Chilean economy.[6] A key factor behind this outcome was the opening of the copper industry to foreign investment, which has expanded Chile's mining production and has avoided the crowding out of (limited) domestic capital from other sectors. At the same time, the existence of foreign ownership has helped to limit the impact of increased copper exports on the real exchange rate (Dutch Disease) and to share the risks of international price fluctuations. Another positive factor for Chile has been the application of a prudent fiscal policy that has led to increased government savings in times of high copper prices. The latter attests to the strong institutional framework in place in Chile to prevent the capture of economic policy by interest groups.[7]

There has been a steady (though slow) diversification of Chilean exports away from nonprocessed natural resources.[8] Overall, there is a considerable preponderance of natural resource–based exports, but there has been a steady increase in the share of products with a more technological content due to the diversification of the country's export basket. In fact, an analysis of merchandise exports reveals a steady but slow diversification over time (Table 8.1).[9] The Herfindahl index on export concentration is still higher in Chile than in representative Latin American countries (Table 8.2), but the gap has been falling. In addition, Chile's export markets have diversified over time, with an increased share from the United States and Asia (Table 8.3). Furthermore, Chile has displayed some ability to reallocate its exports from less dynamic to more dynamic markets.[10]

Recent Evolution of Chilean Exports

One of the concerns about the potential contribution of natural resource–based exports to future growth in Chile refers to the recent slowdown in export growth, and whether it signals structural factors that will also limit export growth in the future.

In fact, the recent evolution of noncopper exports can be clearly linked to the trends of its standard determinants, and there has not been any anomalous break in export behavior. GDP growth of export

---

[3]Tornell (1999).

[4]A key policy implication of this view was the "Prebisch hypothesis," which called for reduced dependency on natural resource exports through a state-led inward-looking industrialization policy based on high tariff and quota barriers (import-substitution industrialization).

[5]Of course, a limited endowment of production factors (particularly human capital) would exacerbate the impact of the exploitation of natural resources on other sectors, but this process could self-perpetuate if the abundance of natural resources slows human capital accumulation by making schooling more expensive. See Asea and Lahiri (1999).

[6]Ilades-Georgetown University and Gerens, Ltd. (1996). This finding is shared by Lagos (1997) and Spilimbergo (1999).

[7]See Section II on Chilean institutions and in particular the description of the country's approaches to maintaining fiscal discipline.

[8]See Appendix I on the evolution of exports in Chile in recent decades.

[9]The latest numbers reflect partly the recent (sharper) fall in copper prices.

[10]For example, Cabezas (2003) showed that one-third of the reduction in exports to Argentina in 2002 was reallocated to other export destinations.

Table 8.1. Evolution of Export Concentration Indicators

	1974–81	1982–89	1990–96	1997–02
Number of items > 0.5 percent of total exports	23	24	28	28
Share in exports of				
Top 5 items	67.5	61.7	56.5	54.5
Top 10 items	77.6	74.5	67.2	65.9
Top 20 items	86.6	85.5	78.3	76.0
Herfindahl index	0.26	0.17	0.12	0.10

Sources: UN COMTRADE database; and author's calculations.

Table 8.2. Selected Countries: Herfindahl Index of Export Concentration

	1974–81	1982–89	1990–96	1997–02
Chile	0.26	0.17	0.12	0.10
Argentina	0.05	0.06	0.04	0.04
Brazil	0.06	0.04	0.03	0.03
Colombia	0.33	0.25	0.09	0.10
Mexico	0.17	0.25	0.08	0.06

Sources: UN COMTRADE database; and author's calculations.

Table 8.3. Chile: Evolution of Export Market Shares
(In percent of total)

	1980	1990	2001	Average Annual Growth Rate
America	38.7	30.1	43.6	7.1
Latin America	24.4	12.5	22.5	6.1
Brazil	9.6	5.6	4.7	3.0
Mexico	1.5	0.7	4.7	12.6
Argentina	6.0	1.3	3.1	3.3
United States	12.6	17.0	19.6	8.8
Canada	1.7	0.7	1.5	5.9
Europe	40.9	39.1	27.8	4.6
European Union	38.7	38.1	25.7	4.5
Asia	18.5	27.0	26.1	8.3
Japan	10.8	16.1	12.1	7.1
China	2.3	0.4	6.1	11.7
Korea	1.5	3.0	3.1	10.4

Sources: Central Bank of Chile; and author's calculations.

Table 8.4. Regression on Noncopper Export Growth

Dependent variable: $D(X\_NC)$
Method: Least squares
Sample (adjusted): 1978–2002

Variable	Coefficient	Standard Error	t-Statistic	Prob.
$D(Y\_XB(-1))$	4.227	1.012	4.176	0.001
$D(REER(-1))$	−0.375	0.138	−2.714	0.014
PX	0.088	0.066	1.328	0.201
C	−0.501	0.334	−1.503	0.150
D81	−0.229	0.055	−4.142	0.001
D82	0.242	0.064	3.786	0.001
D92	0.160	0.051	3.167	0.005
R-squared	0.808	Mean dependent var		0.086
Adjusted R-squared	0.743	S.D. dependent var		0.095
S.E. of regression	0.048	Akaike info criterion		−2.990
Sum squared resid	0.042	Schwarz criterion		−2.649
Log likelihood	44.380	F-statistic		12.591
Durbin-Watson stat	2.339	Prob(F-statistic)		0.000

Residual tests: Breusch-Godfrey = 1.31 (0.52); ARCH = 0.78 (0.38); Jarque-Bera = 2.48 (0.29).

Source: author's calculations.

partners and export prices started to decelerate in the mid-1990s, and the Asian crisis clearly affected Chile's export growth.[11] By contrast, the real exchange rate appreciation in the early 1990s was linked to a deceleration in noncopper exports, but the depreciation in the late 1990s would have helped the recovery in noncopper export growth rates. Noncopper exports and investment flows also appeared to be closely interrelated. A simple econometric estimation of a noncopper export function (Table 8.4) suggests that the weaker export growth in recent years can be explained by the deterioration in external demand and export prices (more than offsetting gains from a more depreciated real exchange rate).[12]

That behavior, however, does not imply that Chile should passively accept changes in external market conditions. International markets are very dynamic, with increasingly tougher demand requirements. This issue is discussed below.

---

[11]Average of percent changes of data for Chile's individual trading partners weighted by their share in total exports of goods, as calculated in the IMF's World Economic Outlook database.

[12]A least-squares estimation was made on first differences since the variables involved were found to be nonstationary and no cointegration relation was detected for the period under analysis (1975–2002). A battery of tests was performed to confirm the stability of parameters and to ensure that the residuals were well behaved. This finding was confirmed in an analysis by Baeza (2003).

Exports and Growth

One of the concerns raised by the literature on natural resource–based exports is founded on a perception of limited links with overall economic activity. This section examines this issue both from an aggregate perspective and by looking at sectoral-level evidence in Chile. The latter offers the strongest evidence of the positive link between natural resource–based exports and economic growth in Chile.

Economic theory argues that openness should increase the level and growth rates of income,[13] however the empirical evidence on the causality link between exports and growth is mixed. Export expansion to foreign markets, by improving resource allocation and production efficiency, can raise the steady-state level of income. On the other hand, exports can become a transmission channel for externalities due to the increased exposure to foreign markets. The endogenous growth models emphasize concepts such as *diffusion of technology* and *learning by doing* as mechanisms that would allow countries to achieve higher steady-state growth rates. Thus, exports allow access to imported capital goods with the latest technological improvements and are themselves forced to innovate to keep and expand access to increasingly demanding foreign markets and create so-called dynamic comparative advan-

---

[13]See Berg and Krueger (2003) on openness and growth.

Table 8.5. Real GDP and Export Volume Growth, Average Per Period
(In percent)

	Real GDP	Export Goods	Export of Goods and Services	Contribution to Growth
1974–81	2.9	10.4	14.4	1.7
1982–89	3.2	7.5	8.0	1.6
1990–96	8.1	10.5	10.4	2.6
1997–2002	3.2	8.0	8.0	2.4

Source: Central Bank of Chile.

tages.[14] The empirical evidence on a cross-country basis tends to confirm this link,[15] but it is less conclusive on a country-by-country basis due in part to *endogeneity* between exports and GDP.

In Chile, exports of goods and services have contributed annually about 2 percentage points to GDP growth since 1974, with the contribution climbing to about 2½ percentage points since the 1990s (Table 8.5). The correlation between exports and GDP growth rates was very high only in the early 1990s, when investment growth rates were historically high. By contrast, in part of the 1980s there was a boost to exports coupled with internal adjustment as a result of the debt crisis, and in recent years the deterioration in terms of trade and in access to international financial markets limited overall GDP growth. The contribution of exports to GDP growth in Chile partly explains the positive growth differential between Chile and other Latin American countries in recent decades (Figure 8.1), which in turn is the result of Chile's significantly larger share of exports in GDP. However, while Chile's integration to the world economy is high by regional standards, the country still lags behind fast-growing economies in South-East Asia (Table 8.6).

As regards the export-led growth hypothesis, a basic cointegration analysis for the period 1975–2002 could not confirm its validity for Chile. Looking at the evolution of exports and GDP over time it can be noticed that in certain periods a strong expansion in exports coexisted with weak nonexportable production; more recently, the expansion in export volumes has not produced a significant rise in employment because technological improvements increased average labor productivity and has been accompanied by sharp falls in export prices (which affected national

Figure 8.1. Differences Between Contribution of Exports to Growth in Chile and Largest Latin American Economies
(Three-year moving averages)

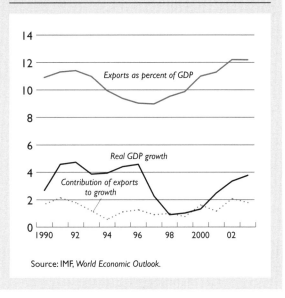

Source: IMF, *World Economic Outlook.*

income growth).[16] An econometric evaluation detected a cointegrating relationship for a system comprising GDP, gross capital formation, and volume of exports, but exports of goods were not found to be weakly exogenous in that estimation (Table 8.7).[17] These results suggest a (long-run) feedback from output (and investment) to exports.[18]

---

[14]See Giles and Williams (2000) for a survey on the empirical literature on the export-led growth hypothesis.

[15]Gallego and Loayza (2002) found a positive impact of openness on output growth in Chile based on a cross-country panel data estimation.

[16]See Central Bank of Chile (2002).

[17]Johansen's procedure for a two-lag (based on Schwarz and Hannan-Quinn criteria) VAR system. Similar results were obtained for a system including noncopper exports volume.

[18]These results contrast with Agosin (1999) time-series analysis for the period 1960–95.

Table 8.6. Selected Economies: Exports and Total Trade Ratios to GDP, Average 1998–2000
(In percent)

	X/GDP	X+M/GDP	Per Capita GDP (In thousands of U.S. dollars)
Singapore	139	263	22,435
Canada	38	71	21,798
Australia	16	33	19,926
New Zealand	24	47	14,080
Taiwan Province of China	44	83	13,057
Korea	38	69	8,419
Argentina	9	18	7,901
Czech Republic	50	104	5,301
Chile	23	45	5,046
Mexico	18	37	4,909
Poland	17	43	4,217
Brazil	8	17	3,885
Malaysia	105	185	3,524
Colombia	14	28	2,205
Thailand	50	92	1,926

Source: IMF, *World Economic Outlook.*

However, sectoral-level data offer the strongest evidence of the link between exports and economic growth in Chile based on spillovers from certain natural resource–based exports to other levels of their production chain and to the development of new export products. A case in point within the agriculture sector is the export of fruits,[19] where Chile was able to transfer, adapt, and extend technologies developed in other countries (with initial assistance from the Corporación de Fomento de la Producción (CORFO)). Afterward, the private sector carried out further innovations at all levels of its production chain (particularly backward linkages) and also disseminated those innovations to other sectors with export potential.

After the trade liberalization process, the manufacturing sector undertook an extensive restructuring centered on (mainly) simpler-technology activities linked to Chile's natural resource endowments.[20] Evidence at the firm level suggests that there had been some technological dynamism, especially in product "engineering" and in adaptation to increasingly rigorous international demand requirements thanks to specialized human capital and the support of specialized institutions (such as the private nonprofit organization Fundación Chile). Specifically, Fundación Chile's initiatives for the development and transfer of new commercial technologies have contributed to the dynamism of agro-industry, fishing, and forestry sectors, including the salmon industry.[21] The latter expanded rapidly in the mid-1990s together with its long chains of upstream and downstream activities (e.g., to feed the fish and distribute medicines, specialized equipment, and rafts in which salmon are grown). A similar process has marked the development of the wine industry, another high-technology sector based on foreign investment and technologies that has gained international recognition and has increased its exports from less than US$100 million in the early 1990s to about US$650 million in 2003.

The Development of New Comparative Advantages

How can the value and diversification in Chilean exports be increased? This section argues that the combination of static comparative advantages with knowledge and innovation should lead to increased value added and diversification, together with a stable macroeconomic framework that provides the right incentives to develop growth-enhancing export

---

[19]Jarvis (1992).
[20]Pietrobelli (1998) and Alvarez and Fuentes (2003).

[21]Fischer (2001). The salmon industry has helped the establishment of newer fishing industries such as for turbot, abalone, and white sturgeon.

Table 8.7. Chile: A Cointegrating Analysis of GDP and Exports

| | Null Hypothesis Summary Test Statistics | | |
	r = 0	r = 1	r = 2
Eigenvalue	0.6512	0.3296	0.2553
Max-Eigenvalue statistic	27.38*	10.40	7.66
5 percent critical value	25.54	18.96	12.25
Trace statistic	45.45*	18.06	7.66
5 percent critical value	42.44	25.32	12.25
	Weak exogeneity test statistics		
Variable	Y	X	I
LR statistic	1.93	5.02*	5.03*
p value	[.16]	[.03]	[.02]
	Multivariate statistics for testing stationarity		
Variable	Y	X	I
LR statistic	16.24**	14.13**	13.69**
	Statistics for testing significance of a given variable		
Variable	Y	X	I
LR statistic	13.42**	11.44**	13.13**

Note: The VAR includes two lags on each variable, an intercept, and dummies for 1982 and 1985. The estimation period is 1974–2002. *(**) denotes rejection of the hypothesis at the 5 percent (1 percent) level.

Source: author's calculations.

sectors. Government supporting policies should be concentrated on improving education levels and on deepening the trade liberalization efforts, particularly by ensuring the access of Chilean products to world markets.

Chile's specialization in natural resource–based exports is in line with its comparative advantage. Chile has plentiful natural resources distributed in extensive latitudinal and altitudinal ranges, a small domestic market, and high transport costs to major international markets. Those structural characteristics have initially led to a specialization in goods with relatively simple production technologies and with relatively high value-added per unit weight.[22] At the same time, and as reviewed in the previous section, there has been a gradual increase in the technological content of exports, and this process has led to the inception of more (and new) differentiated products for international markets. Nonetheless, Chile's export basket varies markedly depending on the geographic destination:[23] there is more natural-resource content in the exports to industrial countries. The latter might be explained by similar natural resource endowment with nonindustrial countries but also by a positive correlation between tariffs and value-added content in Chile's export markets.

There would seem to be benefits from developing new comparative advantages to further diversify the export base and to better respond to changing world demand patterns. There is broad agreement in the literature on the negative correlation between export concentration and growth, partly on account of larger volatility in terms of trade and in the real exchange rate. Even though comparative advantages are key determinants in export patterns, they are not necessarily static and can evolve over time based on the relative supplies of production factors and relative productivity levels. De Ferranti and others (2002) stress that it is not so much *what* a country produces, but *how* it is produced that matters, and that production factors such as knowledge and education should help raise productivity growth, even if a country specializes in "traditional" sectors. In the presence of abundant natural resources, high levels of human capital might not only avoid the crowding out of productive factors to other sectors, but even lead to increased rates of growth, since a well-educated labor facilitates the movement of workers across economic activities and allows the inception of new industrial activities linked to natural resources (Bravo-Ortega and De Gregorio, 2002).

---

[22]Sachs and Larrain (2001).
[23]Zechner (2002) and Ffrench-Davis (2002).

International experience shows the key role of natural resources in the economic success of some natural resource–abundant countries. Many industrial countries based their initial development (and to some extent continue to do so) on their abundant natural resources. The United States' industrial success can be considered as one of the most natural resource–rich nation that made a gradual transition to resource-rich manufacturing industries.[24] Exploitation of minerals in the United States, as in Australia more recently, was the main driving force of growth and industrialization for more than a century.[25] The Nordic countries (which share some characteristics with Chile in terms of geography, market size, and export orientation) also have become highly competitive exporters of manufactures: Sweden and Finland have become leading exporters of telecommunications equipment; Norway has specialized in engineering and shipping services. Two closely interrelated factors stand out behind the success of their development strategies: openness of the economies and high investment in human capital. The latter helped those countries to absorb technological progress to transform resource-based activities into industries with higher productivity levels.

By contrast, inward-oriented policies and high tariffs have not helped economic growth. Irwin (2002) shows that inward-oriented policies and high tariffs were not a critical factor behind the late nineteenth century growth experience of high-income countries. Noland (2001) suggests that industrial policies made at most a minor contribution to the recent growth experience in East Asia, and that most of its success came from good macroeconomic policies, export orientation, and investment in human capital and in efficient social infrastructure. In Latin America, industrial policies and/or import substitution seemed to work at the beginning but started to disintegrate by the 1960s, partly because of the pressures of interest groups to keep incentives indefinitely; furthermore, several Latin American countries used receipts from natural resource exports to finance industrial policies and protectionism, causing a systematic overvaluation of local currencies and a misallocation of resources that might explain the negative association of natural resource abundance and growth rates.

Accumulation of Human Capital and Technological Innovation

Chile's market-oriented policies,[26] its stable macroeconomic framework, and its open foreign direct investment (FDI) regime should continue to provide adequate incentives to develop growth-enhancing export sectors, but the country could make the most out of those exports by developing abilities to innovate and absorb innovation. The general framework of policies provides incentives for an efficient allocation of resources. However, the technological content of Chile's export basket is still not very high. A channel to absorb technology and to innovate is FDI; in this area Chile has been actively signing bilateral treaties with its main investor countries and regions, while the free trade agreements with large external partners could help Chile become a "hub" for multinational corporations to access larger neighboring Latin American countries.[27] However, there is evidence that foreign companies establishing in outward-oriented countries tend to use production technologies that fit the host country's comparative advantage.[28]

The accumulation of human capital is the key channel of technological innovation and assimilation, and an essential requirement for a succesful export-led economic growth.[29]

- There has been significant progress in educational attainment of the labor force, but even though Chile is in the upper range of educational attainment of Latin America's labor force (7.9 years of schooling in 2000, Figure 8.2), it still lags compared with natural resource–abundant member countries of the Organization for Economic Cooperation and Development (OECD) (11.1 years) and East Asian tigers (9.7 years).[30]

- Schooling attainment levels do not reveal the adequacy of education: a study on adult literacy skills[31] showed that 50 percent of Chile's labor force has a low level of basic reading comprehension and only 20 percent achieved the level considered "adequate."[32]

---

macroeconomic environment index, and nineteenth in the public institutions index (first in Latin America). More recently, the government established a special tax treatment (no double taxation) for firms using Chile as a regional investment platform.

[27]See Appendix II on Chile's trade policy strategy and the characteristics of recent free trade agreements.

[28]De Ferranti and others (2003).

[29]The critical importance of educational levels in achieving higher growth rates was highlighted in a cross-country panel data regression by Gallego and Loayza (2002): increases in average years of schooling and in the quality of education in Chile to the top 10 percent of the world would lead to a rise in per capita growth rates of 2 percentage points, to 6 percent.

[30]Brunner and Elacqua (2003) provide an assessment of human capital in Chile.

[31]IALS, published by the OECD, as mentioned in Arellano (2001).

[32]To "cope with the demands of everyday life and work in a complex society."

---

[24]Irwin (2002).

[25]Wright and Czelusta (2002).

[26]Chile ranked twentieth among 80 countries in the *Global Competitiveness Report* 2002–2003, thirteenth in the specific

Figure 8.2. Selected Economies: Educational Attainment and Income

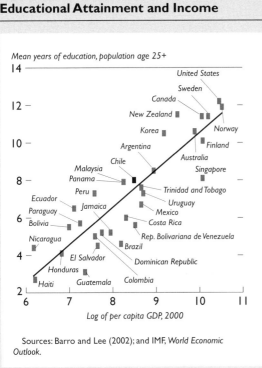

Sources: Barro and Lee (2002); and IMF, *World Economic Outlook*.

Figure 8.3. Selected Economies: TIMSS Mathematics Results and Income, 1999

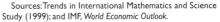
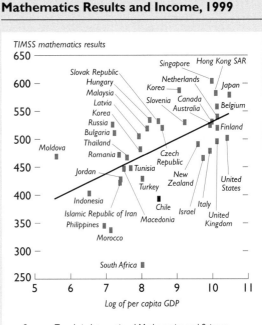

Sources: Trends in International Mathematics and Science Study (1999); and IMF, *World Economic Outlook*.

• An analysis of the quality of current education based on the results of the 1999 international study of student achievement in mathematics and science (TIMSS) suggests relatively low quality (even adjusting for income levels, Figure 8.3): Chile ranked thirty-fifth among the 38 countries that participated in the study.[33] Part of the poor outcome in international tests can be traced to Chile's higher income inequality (Figure 8.4).[34]

The government could help improve the quality of education by updating curricula, improving teachers' skills, tracking performance, and improving accreditation systems.[35] Total (public and private) spending is high compared with countries with similar income levels. The fact that Chile spends relatively more but achieves lower outcomes than, for

Figure 8.4. Selected Economies: TIMSS Mathematics Results and Inequality in Income, 1999

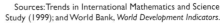
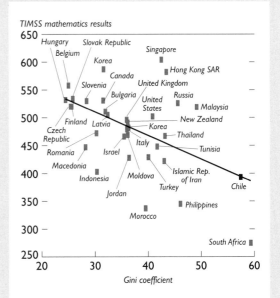

Sources: Trends in International Mathematics and Science Study (1999); and World Bank, *World Development Indicators*.

---

[33]In the microeconomic competitiveness ranking of the GCR, Chile was placed about sixtieth in quality of mathematics and science education and of public schools among 80 countries surveyed.

[34]The differences in performance take place between schools, which in turn are segmented by socioeconomic characteristics. Cuadernos de Economía (2002).

[35]World Bank (2004) and De Ferranti and others (2003).

Table 8.8. Export Volume and Average Growth Rates
(In percent)

	1986–89	1990–96	1997–2002
Agriculture, hunting, forestry, and fishing	12.0	8.4	4.2
Mining	4.7	9.1	6.9
Manufacturing	15.4	13.3	7.3
Total exports	9.0	10.2	7.1
Copper	3.5	9.6	7.9
Noncopper	13.1	11.1	6.0

Source: Central Bank of Chile.

example, Mexico, suggests that the emphasis should be placed on increasing efficiency of spending and quality of education. The Chilean government has been undertaking several efforts in this area, including an increased focus on preschool education, increase in school hours, the review of curricula, and the introduction of standardized admission tests to tertiary education. The World Bank is also assisting in the design of programs to better match labor force skills with the needs of a knowledge-based economy. Increased accountability by public (municipal) and subsidized (through the voucher system for education) private schools should help tackle educational inequalities across income strata; an initiative that might also be considered is to make variable the value of vouchers to broaden students' choices and increase competition within the educational system.

Some other microeconomic reforms might also help encourage private sector innovation.[36] The government could transfer most of its research execution (often disconnected from the needs of the private sector) to the private sector (through bidding processes), strengthen intellectual property rights, and improve patent approval procedures.

Appendix I: Evolution of Exports in Chile

Exports in Chile have been very dynamic in recent decades, but have decelerated somewhat in recent years. Since 1980, the value of exports has tripled in real terms and the volume of exports has quintupled, substantially above world trends. The increase in the volume of exports has averaged more than 9 percent in the past 30 years, and has been broadly based (Table 8.8). However, the expansion of exports has decelerated recently. Growth in export value (in real

[36]See World Bank (2004).

terms) has been far more volatile owing to sharp fluctuations in export prices.

The structure of exports has been dominated by natural resources. As shown in Table 8.9 (which includes refined copper as a nonprocessed natural resource, ignoring embedded technological improvements), exports of natural resources and processed natural resources have accounted for more than 85 percent of total exports.

The performance of exports has partly resulted from an export-oriented policy framework that included an aggressive trade liberalization process, a competitive real exchange rate, and several (temporary) export support schemes.

- Starting in the mid-1970s, exports expanded following an aggressive trade liberalization process (through reduced tariffs and elimination of quantitative restrictions) and the utilization of excess capacity in the export sector.

- After the debt crisis of the early 1980s, exports experienced an increased dynamism on account of a substantial real depreciation and the introduction of several export support schemes, including subsidies (simplified drawback system for nontraditional exports, delayed payment of tariffs on imported capital goods, and tax incentives for the forestry sector), financing facilities (through CORFO), institutional support for export activities (ProChile and Fundación Chile), and incentives for foreign direct investment (*Chapter 19* on debt-equity swaps).

- In the 1990s, exports benefited from the consolidation of a sound macroeconomic framework and a trade policy strategy geared toward the negotiation of regional trade agreements to improve market access for Chilean exports (in the context of the phasing out of export subsidies as agreed with the World Trade Organization (WTO)).

Table 8.9. Export Structure
(In percent of total)

	1975	1986	1995	2002
Natural resources	74.8	70.2	57.5	51.1
Processed natural resources	18.2	25.4	33.5	34.6
Other industrial products	6.9	4.5	9.0	14.2

Sources: Central Bank of Chile; and author's calculations.

Appendix II: Chile's Trade Policy Strategy and Recent Agreements

Starting in the mid-1970s, Chile pursued an export-oriented development strategy, eliminating the antiexport bias of trade policy by means of aggressive unilateral trade liberalization.[37] Tariffs were lowered sharply and set at a uniform rate for all imports except a few agricultural products that were subject to price bands. The uniform tariff was reduced from 15 percent to 11 percent in June 1991, and even further to 6 percent over the period 1999–2003. The unilateral trade liberalization—together with macroeconomic stability, a "competitive" real exchange rate, and several specific export promotion programs[38]—contributed to the significant expansion and diversification of exports.

Chile has actively participated in multilateral trade negotiations within the framework of the WTO and in 1995 incorporated the WTO Agreements into its domestic legislation. The government considers that subscription to the WTO, despite limited progress in the liberalization of important sectors (e.g., agriculture, textiles, and clothing), benefits Chile's exports by strengthening the dispute settlement mechanism, adopting a common set of rules that reduce trade distortions, improving the quality of information regarding market access, and promoting investment flows through clear rules for trade in services and in intellectual property matters.[39] Domestically, the adoption of WTO-consistent legislation should reduce the possibility of adopting discriminatory protectionist policies and reinforce trade-related institutions. The WTO-tariff bound agreed to by Chile is 25 percent for most products, 31.5 percent for some

agricultural products (wheat, wheat flour, oils, and dairy products), and 98 percent for sugar.

Since the early 1990s, Chile's trade policy has focused on the negotiation of a number of regional (both bilateral and plurilateral) integration agreements (RIAs). This policy has been characterized by the authorities as "open regionalism," complementary to the multilateral trade strategy and aimed at ensuring niches for Chilean exports.[40] Under the auspices of the Latin American Integration Association (LAIA), Chile signed economic complementarity agreements with Mexico (1991), República Bolivariana de Venezuela (1993), Colombia (1993), Ecuador (1994), Mercosur (1996), and Peru (1998), and a partial-scope agreement with Bolivia (1993).[41] Chile signed a free trade agreement with Canada in 1996,[42] and concluded negotiations for free trade agreements with the European Union (EU), the United States, and Korea in 2002, and with the European Free Trade Association (EFTA) in early 2003.

The Rationale for Regionalism

In the economic literature, regionalism entails second-best type policies and no general theorem exists to support it. According to the standard trade theory, there is no additional benefit that could not be achieved through unilateral liberalization.[43] Assuming perfect competition, small economies, constant

---

[37]Until the early 1970s, Chile had a heavily regulated economy based on an import-substitution development strategy. In fact, the average tariff in 1973 was 105 percent and ranged from 0 percent to 750 percent, in addition to some quantitative restrictions.

[38]For a detailed review of those policies, see Agosin (1999) and Macario (1998).

[39]World Trade Organization (1997).

[40]World Trade Organization (1997).

[41]The agreements with Mexico, Venezuela, Colombia, and Ecuador aimed at establishing free trade for about 95 percent of all tariff lines by 2000. The agreement with Mercosur would establish free trade for at least 75 percent of tariff lines by early 2006 and free trade for all tariff lines by 2014. The agreements also included provisions for the liberalization of investments, establishment of transparent rules for applying safeguard clauses, and commitments to harmonize export incentives.

[42]The agreement with Canada, which entered into force in July 1997, provided for the elimination of most tariffs by January 2003, with the exception of tariffs on some "sensitive" agricultural products, which would be phased out until 2014.

[43]Velasco and Tokman (1993).

returns of scale and no transport costs, efficiency in production and consumption is achieved when tariffs (and nontariff barriers) are zero, even if trading partners do not reciprocate. In this context, increased exports from RIAs do not increase welfare as the resulting producer surplus would be zero. Growth enhancement through the adoption of technological knowledge (following the literature based on endogenous growth theory) could be achieved through unilateral trade liberalization and not only by agreements with developed countries (major producers of technological knowledge). In addition, uniform tariffs (which do not exist in practice under the presence of RIAs) have the advantages of equal effective protection rates across sectors, simplicity that reduces business costs, lower customs administration costs (no need for rules of origin), and lower discretion (with lower incentives for corruption).

Regarding specific costs of RIAs, obviously the most important is related to *trade diversion*, as preferential treatments might lead to welfare-reducing distortions in production and consumption. The cost of trade diversion depends on the level of overall protection and the advantages that RIAs' partners are given. For instance, RIAs with small, developing countries are likely to reduce welfare (as shown for the agreement with Mercosur by Harrison, Rutherford, and Tarr (2002)) as they tend to be based on political considerations. On the other hand, developing countries have limited bargaining power in their negotiations of RIAs with the United States and the EU. Hence, some conditions to get an RIA might be tough in areas such as intellectual property rights (e.g., patent protection on pharmaceuticals before 1991 given the abundance of generic products) and environmental and labor standards. The latter might reduce the flexibility of the economy, which precisely might be needed to facilitate the adjustment to the RIA. Another cost of RIAs involves the need to establish rules of origin to avoid the problem of *trade deflection*; those rules can in turn lead to additional trade diversion and welfare loss as they are typically hard to enforce, particularly in the presence of overlapping RIAs.[44]

Chile's policymakers support the regionalist approach on several grounds:

- Improved market access for Chilean exports and economies of scale that lead to increased efficiency.[45] Through several RIAs Chile will have lowered its preferential tariff to all its major trading partners, with an effect similar to that of uni-

lateral trade liberalization, but with better market access for its export products. In addition, negotiations would allow access for products with higher value added, which tend to be subject to tariff escalations, a factor that has complicated the diversification of exports away from natural resources.[46]

- Protection against potential establishment of protectionist measures, thereby ensuring the stability of exports. For example, the Generalized System of Preferences (GSP) gives preferential access to the U.S. market but benefits have to be renewed from time to time and can be eliminated unilaterally. RIAs normally establish dispute settlement mechanisms to increase confidence in the security of market access.

- RIAs in Chile result in relatively low trade diversion costs, since Chile has a low uniform tariff and RIAs do not include nontariff restrictions to the rest of the world.

- Regionalist strategy is a response to limited progress in multilateral negotiations sponsored by the WTO.

- Strategy is a response to the formation of trade blocs. Being excluded is costly as in the case of the North American Free Trade Agreement, since Mexico and Canada are the most important competitors of Chile as providers of natural resources and processed natural resources to the U.S. market.[47] By contrast, when signing several RIAs a country becomes a "hub," and its partners become "spokes," if they have not signed free trade agreements with each other. In that case, investors would prefer to invest in the hub, reaching the spokes from there.

- The negotiation of RIAs tends to involve multidimensional aspects complementary to trade relations. For example, in the agreement with Canada (1996) both countries decided to eschew antidumping actions against each other. In addition, RIAs normally include specific provisions to promote and protect investment flows between trading partners. The latter would benefit Chile as a recipient of foreign direct investment flows from developed countries and as an investor in other South American countries.

---

[44]Krueger (1997).

[45]The unilateral trade liberalization strategy implicitly assumes that the tariff and nontariff barriers facing the exports of a country are very low or nonexistent (Wonnacott and Wonnacott, 1981).

[46]Harrison, Rutherford, and Tarr (2002) show that the strategy of combining free trade agreements with Canada, Mexico, the United States, the EU, Mercosur, and the rest of South America produces welfare gains for Chile that are many multiples of the value of unilateral free trade if it were to attain tariff-free access to all these markets.

[47]Campero and Escobar (1992), Zechner (2002), and Schiff (2002).

- Negotiation of RIAs could be adapted to the perceived sectoral and regional costs and benefits. In fact, it could be argued that the sequencing of Chile's RIAs (by concentrating on neighboring countries first) allowed Chile to strengthen some of its industries before signing agreements with developed countries (Selaive, 1998). In addition, longer phase-out periods were agreed on for sensitive agricultural products.[48]

- RIAs with developed countries should raise credibility of the overall policy framework and governance, helping to differentiate Chile from other countries.

Recent Regional Trade Agreements

As mentioned earlier, Chile concluded negotiations for free trade agreements with the EU, the United States, and Korea in 2002, and with the EFTA in early 2003. These countries account for about half of Chile's exports.

Chile's agreement with the EU is the first one signed by a Latin American country and also the most advanced trade deal the EU has ever negotiated with a nonmember country. This means that, in addition to better access for Chile's export products, there would be an incentive for European investors to establish businesses in Chile as an entry to the other Latin American countries. Under this agreement, about 85 percent of Chilean exports to the EU would enjoy zero tariff from the beginning, and this share would increase to 96 percent after 4 years and to 99.7 percent after 10 years.[49] An important feature is the phaseout of tariff escalation clauses that historically have hindered diversification of Chilean exports to the EU.[50] Before the agreement, the fishing and wine industries were facing 13 percent and 10 percent tariffs, respectively, while agro-industrial exports faced tariffs of 40 percent. The agreement also covers investment and services, establishes a dispute resolution mechanism, and reduces sanitary and phytosanitary inspections on Chilean exports by accepting the reports from the relevant Chilean regulatory agencies. The trade agreement with the EU took effect in February 2003. Tariff reductions agreed to for goods have already been applied, while those for services and investment would take effect only after the agreement's approval by the parliaments of each EU member country. A general equilibrium study reported by the central bank estimated the potential *direct* impact of the agreement on Chilean exports and GDP at 3.2 percent and 0.5 percent, respectively.[51]

The agreement with the United States includes trade, a dispute resolution mechanism, services, investment, and sections on environmental and labor standards. The agreement was signed in June 2003 and was ratified by the United States and Chilean congresses, and went into effect in January 2004. The agreement on trade consolidates the market access conditions for Chilean exports (including GSP conditions) and aims at eliminating all tariffs in a maximum period of 12 years, including on agricultural and textile products. About 87 percent of Chilean exports to the United States would enjoy zero tariff from the beginning, and about 95 percent will be completely liberalized in 10–12 years. All escalation tariffs on Chilean exports will be gradually phased out, while tariffs on textile products are to be eliminated immediately. On capital flows, the agreement states that foreign investors will only be able to protest against restrictive measures by the Chilean government (on payments and transfers as well as on inflows) only a year after their implementation; this feature would allow Chile to put in place transitory restrictive measures to regulate the movement of capital flows. Consultation mechanisms will be established on environmental and labor issues, with the commitment of both countries to comply with current relevant regulations in that area that are consistent with internationally approved standards. Based on estimates by the Chilean Ministry of Foreign Relations, the potential *direct* impact of the trade agreement (assuming complete liberalization) on Chilean exports and GDP would be 16 percent and 2 percent, respectively.

The free trade agreement with Korea in October 2002 is the first one agreed upon between an Asian and a Western economy, and between transpacific members of the Asia-Pacific Economic Community (APEC). It is still being drafted into law; there is no

---

[48]Hachette and Morales (1996) provide evidence that the agricultural sector would be the most affected (both on the positive and negative sides) by free trade agreements, but they also note the capacity that the agricultural sector had shown in the past to restructure itself.

[49]Chilean exports to the EU could enjoy this treatment only up to certain quotas of total export to the EU area, but these quotas are so large (larger than the total trade with the EU), and growing at about 10 percent a year, that it is unlikely they could ever become binding. The remaining share (0.3 percent) would be subject to a revision clause.

[50]For instance, export concentration levels to the EU are far higher than to the rest of the world, with exports of processed natural resources (particularly refined copper) accounting for about 73 percent of total exports to the EU.

[51]General equilibrium model from "Sustainable Impact Assessment" SIA-Chile, referred to in the Central Bank's Monetary Policy Report (January 2003). However, these estimates are static and conservative since they do not consider other channels, such as better resource allocation, reduced transaction costs, lower uncertainty on policies, and a better business climate, all of which would tend to motivate investment in physical and human capital and productivity-enhancing technological exchanges.

specific timetable for the legislation to be discussed in both countries' legislatures, but it would likely be enacted into law in 2004. Tariffs on Chilean exports would be eliminated in six steps over the next 13 years, with tariffs on 41 percent of exports being eliminated immediately and on 97 percent of exports in the next 7 years.[52] This should benefit Chilean exporters vis-à-vis their main competitors in the Korean market, that is, Canada and New Zealand. In addition, the current export basket to Korea is not very diversified and the negotiated tariff reductions would open opportunities for new exports in the agriculture, forestry, fishing, wood, and chemical sectors. This agreement would also open opportunities for Korean investments in Chile aimed at an expanded Latin American market.

The agreement with EFTA also includes a dispute resolution mechanism, removal of antidumping measures, and sections on services and investment. The trade agreement involves the immediate abolition of tariffs for more than 90 percent of Chilean exports.

References

Agosin, M., 1999, "Comercio y Crecimiento en Chile," *Revista de la CEPAL*, No. 68 (August), pp. 79–100.

Alvarez, R., and R. Fuentes, 2003, "Trade Reforms and Manufacturing Industry in Chile," Central Bank of Chile Working Paper No. 210 (Santiago: Central Bank of Chile).

Arellano, J.P., 2001, "International Competitiveness and Education in Latin America and the Caribbean Countries," in *The Latin American Competitiveness Report 2001–2002*, World Economic Forum (Geneva).

Asea, P., and A. Lahiri, 1999, "The Precious Bane," *Journal of Economic Dynamics and Control*, Vol. 23, No. 5–6 (April), pp. 823–49.

Auty, R., 1990, *Resource-Based Industrialization: Sowing the Oil in Eight Developing Countries* (Oxford: Clarendon Press).

Baeza, W., 2003, "Exportaciones y PIB Socios" (unpublished; Santiago: Central Bank of Chile).

Barro, R.J., and J.-W. Lee, 2002, "International Measures of Schooling Years and Schooling Quality" [data set]. Available via the Internet at http://www.worldbank.org/research/growth/ddbarle2.htm.

Berg, A., and A. Krueger, 2003, "Trade, Growth, and Poverty: A Selective Study," IMF Working Paper No. 03/30 (Washington: International Monetary Fund).

Bravo-Ortega, C., and J. De Gregorio, 2002, "The Relative Richness of the Poor? Natural Resources, Human Capital and Economic Growth," Central Bank of Chile Working Paper No. 139 (Santiago: Central Bank of Chile).

Brunner, J., and G. Elacqua, 2003, *Informe: Capital Humano en Chile* (Santiago: Univ. Adolfo Ibáñez).

Cabezas, M., 2003, "Disminución de las Exportaciones a Argentina" (unpublished; Santiago: Central Bank of Chile).

Campero, M.P., and B. Escobar, 1992, "Evolución y Composición de las Exportaciones Chilenas, 1986–1991," CIEPLAN.

Central Bank of Chile, Monetary Policy Report, various issues (Santiago).

Cuadernos de Economía, 2002, "La Economía de la Educación y el Sistema Educativo Chileno," Vol. 39, No. 118, Special Issue (December).

De Ferranti, and others, 2002, *From Natural Resources to the Knowledge Economy: Trade and Job Quality* (Washington: World Bank).

———, 2003, *Closing the Gap in Education and Technology* (Washington: World Bank).

Ffrench-Davis, R., 2002, "El Impacto de las Exportaciones sobre el Crecimiento en Chile," *Revista de la CEPAL* No. 76 (April), pp. 143–60.

Fischer, R., 2001, "Trade Liberalization, Development and Government Policy in Chile" (unpublished).

———, and P. Meller, 1999, "Latin American Trade Regime Reforms and Perceptions" (unpublished; Santiago: Universidad de Chile).

Gallego, F., and N. Loayza, 2002, "The Golden Period for Growth in Chile: Explanations and Forecast," Central Bank of Chile Working Paper No. 146 (Santiago: Central Bank of Chile).

Gelb, A., and others, 1988, *Oil Windfall: Blessing or Curse?* (New York: Oxford University Press).

Giles, J.A., and C.L. Williams, 2000, "Export-Led Growth: A Survey of the Empirical Literature and Some Non-Causality Results," *Journal of International Trade and Economic Development*, Vol. 9, No. 4 (December), pp. 445–70.

Hachette, D., and G. Morales, 1996, "Impactos Regionales del Nafta y Mercosur," *Estudios Públicos*, No. 63.

Harrison, G., T. Rutherford, and D. Tarr, 2002, "Trade Policy Options for Chile: The Importance of Market Access," *World Bank Economic Review*, Vol. 16, No. 1, pp. 49–79.

Ilades-Georgetown University and Gerens Ltd, 1996, "The Copper Boom in the Chilean Economy: What Should We Expect?"(Santiago).

Irwin, D.A., 2002, "Did Import Substitution Promote Growth in the Late Nineteenth Century?" NBER Working Paper No. 8751 (Cambridge, Massachusetts: National Bureau of Economic Research).

Jarvis, L., 1992, "Cambios en los Roles de los Sectores Público y Privado en el Desarrollo Tecnológico: Lecciones a Partir del Sector Frutícola Chileno," *Colección Estudios CIEPLAN*, No. 36 (December), pp. 5–39.

Krueger, A.O., 1997, "Problems with Overlapping Free Trade Areas," in *Regionalism Versus Multilateral Trade Arrangements*, ed. by T. Ito and A.O. Krueger (Chicago: University of Chicago Press).

Lagos, G., 1997, "Developing National Mining Policies in Chile: 1974–96," *Resources Policy*, Vol. 23 (June), pp. 51–69.

---

[52]Both parties agreed on a list of sensitive products that will be exempted altogether from the free trade agreement.

Lederman, D., and W. Maloney, 2002, "Open Questions About the Link Between Natural Resources and Economic Growth: Sachs and Warner Revisited" (unpublished; Washington: World Bank).

Macario, C., 1998, "Chile: From Policies That Subsidize Exports to Policies That Enhance Competitiveness," *Integration and Trade*, Vol. 2, No. 4–5 (January–August), pp. 115–32.

Martin, W., and D. Mitra, 1999, "Productivity Growth and Convergence in Agriculture and Manufacturing," Policy Research Working Paper No. 2171 (Washington: World Bank).

Noland, M., 2001, "Industrial Policies and Growth: Lessons for International Experience" (unpublished).

Oliveira, J., and T. Price, 2002, "International Competitiveness in Argentina, Brazil and Chile: The Role of Policies and Market Structures" (unpublished; Paris: Organization for Economic Cooperation and Development).

Pietrobelli, C., 1998, *Industry, Competitiveness, and Technological Capabilities in Chile: A New Tiger from Latin America?* (Houndmills, Basingstoke, Hampshire: Macmillan Press Ltd.; New York: St. Martin's Press).

Sachs, J., and F. Larrain, 2001, "A Structural Analysis of Chile's Long-Term Growth: History, Prospects and Policy Implications" (unpublished).

Sachs, J., and A. Warner, 1995, "Natural Resource Abundance and Economic Growth," NBER Working Paper No. 5398 (Cambridge, Massachusetts: National Bureau of Economic Research).

Schiff, M., 2002, "Chile's Trade Policy: An Assessment," Central Bank of Chile Working Paper No. 151 (Santiago: Central Bank of Chile).

Selaive, J., 1998, "Comercio Intraindustrial en Chile," Central Bank of Chile Working Paper No. 44 (Santiago: Central Bank of Chile).

Spilimbergo, A., 1999, "Copper and the Chilean Economy: 1960–98," IMF Working Paper No. 99/57 (Washington: International Monetary Fund).

Tornell, A., 1999, "The Voracity Effect," *American Economic Review*, Vol. 89 (March), pp. 22–46.

Velasco, A., and M. Tokman, 1993, "Opciones para la Política Comercial Chilena en los 90," *Estudios Públicos* No., 52.

Wonnacott, P., and R. Wonnacott, 1981, "Is Unilateral Tariff Reduction Preferable to a Customs Union? The Curious Case of the Missing Foreign Tariffs," *American Economic Review*, Vol. 71, No. 4 (September), pp. 704–14.

World Bank, 2004, *Chile: New Economy Study*, Report No. 25666-CL (Washington).

World Economic Forum, *Global Competitiveness Report*, various issues (Geneva).

World Trade Organization, 1997, *Trade Policy Review Mechanism: Chile* (Geneva).

Wright, G., and J. Czelusta, 2002, "Exorcizing the Resource Curse: Minerals as a Knowledge Industry, Past and Present" (unpublished; Stanford, California: Stanford University).

Zechner, C., 2002, *Expanding NAFTA: Economic Effects on Chile of Free Trade with the United States* (Munster; London: Lit).

Recent Occasional Papers of the International Monetary Fund

231. Chile: Institutions and Policies Underpinning Stability and Growth, by Eliot Kalter, Steven Phillips, Marco A. Espinosa-Vega, Rodolfo Luzio, Mauricio Villafuerte, and Manmohan Singh. 2004.

230. Financial Stability in Dollarized Countries, by Anne-Marie Gulde, David Hoelscher, Alain Ize, David Marston, and Gianni De Nicoló. 2004.

229. Evolution and Performance of Exchange Rate Regimes, by Kenneth S. Rogoff, Aasim M. Husain, Ashoka Mody, Robin Brooks, and Nienke Oomes. 2004.

228. Capital Markets and Financial Intermediation in The Baltics, by Alfred Schipke, Christian Beddies, Susan M. George, and Niamh Sheridan. 2004.

227. U.S. Fiscal Policies and Priorities for Long-Run Sustainability, Martin Mühleisen and Christopher Towe, editors. 2004.

226. Hong Kong SAR: Meeting the Challenges of Integration with the Mainland, edited by Eswar Prasad, with contributions from Jorge Chan-Lau, Dora Iakova, William Lee, Hong Liang, Ida Liu, Papa N'Diaye, and Tao Wang. 2004.

225. Rules-Based Fiscal Policy in France, Germany, Italy, and Spain, by Teresa Dában, Enrica Detragiache, Gabriel di Bella, Gian Maria Milesi-Ferretti, and Steven Symansky. 2003.

224. Managing Systemic Banking Crises, by a staff team led by David S. Hoelscher and Marc Quintyn. 2003.

223. Monetary Union Among Member Countries of the Gulf Cooperation Council, by a staff team led by Ugo Fasano. 2003.

222. Informal Funds Transfer Systems: An Analysis of the Informal Hawala System, by Mohammed El Qorchi, Samuel Munzele Maimbo, and John F. Wilson. 2003.

221. Deflation: Determinants, Risks, and Policy Options, by Manmohan S. Kumar. 2003.

220. Effects of Financial Globalization on Developing Countries: Some Empirical Evidence, by Eswar S. Prasad, Kenneth Rogoff, Shang-Jin Wei, and Ayhan Kose. 2003.

219. Economic Policy in a Highly Dollarized Economy: The Case of Cambodia, by Mario de Zamaroczy and Sopanha Sa. 2003.

218. Fiscal Vulnerability and Financial Crises in Emerging Market Economies, by Richard Hemming, Michael Kell, and Axel Schimmelpfennig. 2003.

217. Managing Financial Crises: Recent Experience and Lessons for Latin America, edited by Charles Collyns and G. Russell Kincaid. 2003.

216. Is the PRGF Living Up to Expectations?—An Assessment of Program Design, by Sanjeev Gupta, Mark Plant, Benedict Clements, Thomas Dorsey, Emanuele Baldacci, Gabriela Inchauste, Shamsuddin Tareq, and Nita Thacker. 2002.

215. Improving Large Taxpayers' Compliance: A Review of Country Experience, by Katherine Baer. 2002.

214. Advanced Country Experiences with Capital Account Liberalization, by Age Bakker and Bryan Chapple. 2002.

213. The Baltic Countries: Medium-Term Fiscal Issues Related to EU and NATO Accession, by Johannes Mueller, Christian Beddies, Robert Burgess, Vitali Kramarenko, and Joannes Mongardini. 2002.

212. Financial Soundness Indicators: Analytical Aspects and Country Practices, by V. Sundararajan, Charles Enoch, Armida San José, Paul Hilbers, Russell Krueger, Marina Moretti, and Graham Slack. 2002.

211. Capital Account Liberalization and Financial Sector Stability, by a staff team led by Shogo Ishii and Karl Habermeier. 2002.

210. IMF-Supported Programs in Capital Account Crises, by Atish Ghosh, Timothy Lane, Marianne Schulze-Ghattas, Aleš Bulíř, Javier Hamann, and Alex Mourmouras. 2002.

209. Methodology for Current Account and Exchange Rate Assessments, by Peter Isard, Hamid Faruqee, G. Russell Kincaid, and Martin Fetherston. 2001.

208. Yemen in the 1990s: From Unification to Economic Reform, by Klaus Enders, Sherwyn Williams, Nada Choueiri, Yuri Sobolev, and Jan Walliser. 2001.

207. Malaysia: From Crisis to Recovery, by Kanitta Meesook, Il Houng Lee, Olin Liu, Yougesh Khatri, Natalia Tamirisa, Michael Moore, and Mark H. Krysl. 2001.

206. The Dominican Republic: Stabilization, Structural Reform, and Economic Growth, by a staff team led by Philip Young comprising Alessandro Giustiniani, Werner C. Keller, and Randa E. Sab and others. 2001.

205. Stabilization and Savings Funds for Nonrenewable Resources, by Jeffrey Davis, Rolando Ossowski, James Daniel, and Steven Barnett. 2001.

204. Monetary Union in West Africa (ECOWAS): Is It Desirable and How Could It Be Achieved? by Paul Masson and Catherine Pattillo. 2001.

203. Modern Banking and OTC Derivatives Markets: The Transformation of Global Finance and Its Implications for Systemic Risk, by Garry J. Schinasi, R. Sean Craig, Burkhard Drees, and Charles Kramer. 2000.

202. Adopting Inflation Targeting: Practical Issues for Emerging Market Countries, by Andrea Schaechter, Mark R. Stone, and Mark Zelmer. 2000.

201. Developments and Challenges in the Caribbean Region, by Samuel Itam, Simon Cueva, Erik Lundback, Janet Stotsky, and Stephen Tokarick. 2000.

200. Pension Reform in the Baltics: Issues and Prospects, by Jerald Schiff, Niko Hobdari, Axel Schimmelpfennig, and Roman Zytek. 2000.

199. Ghana: Economic Development in a Democratic Environment, by Sérgio Pereira Leite, Anthony Pellechio, Luisa Zanforlin, Girma Begashaw, Stefania Fabrizio, and Joachim Harnack. 2000.

198. Setting Up Treasuries in the Baltics, Russia, and Other Countries of the Former Soviet Union: An Assessment of IMF Technical Assistance, by Barry H. Potter and Jack Diamond. 2000.

197. Deposit Insurance: Actual and Good Practices, by Gillian G.H. Garcia. 2000.

196. Trade and Trade Policies in Eastern and Southern Africa, by a staff team led by Arvind Subramanian, with Enrique Gelbard, Richard Harmsen, Katrin Elborgh-Woytek, and Piroska Nagy. 2000.

195. The Eastern Caribbean Currency Union—Institutions, Performance, and Policy Issues, by Frits van Beek, José Roberto Rosales, Mayra Zermeño, Ruby Randall, and Jorge Shepherd. 2000.

194. Fiscal and Macroeconomic Impact of Privatization, by Jeffrey Davis, Rolando Ossowski, Thomas Richardson, and Steven Barnett. 2000.

193. Exchange Rate Regimes in an Increasingly Integrated World Economy, by Michael Mussa, Paul Masson, Alexander Swoboda, Esteban Jadresic, Paolo Mauro, and Andy Berg. 2000.

192. Macroprudential Indicators of Financial System Soundness, by a staff team led by Owen Evans, Alfredo M. Leone, Mahinder Gill, and Paul Hilbers. 2000.

191. Social Issues in IMF-Supported Programs, by Sanjeev Gupta, Louis Dicks-Mireaux, Ritha Khemani, Calvin McDonald, and Marijn Verhoeven. 2000.

190. Capital Controls: Country Experiences with Their Use and Liberalization, by Akira Ariyoshi, Karl Habermeier, Bernard Laurens, İnci Ötker-Robe, Jorge Iván Canales Kriljenko, and Andrei Kirilenko. 2000.

189. Current Account and External Sustainability in the Baltics, Russia, and Other Countries of the Former Soviet Union, by Donal McGettigan. 2000.

188. Financial Sector Crisis and Restructuring: Lessons from Asia, by Carl-Johan Lindgren, Tomás J.T. Baliño, Charles Enoch, Anne-Marie Gulde, Marc Quintyn, and Leslie Teo. 1999.

187. Philippines: Toward Sustainable and Rapid Growth, Recent Developments and the Agenda Ahead, by Markus Rodlauer, Prakash Loungani, Vivek Arora, Charalambos Christofides, Enrique G. De la Piedra, Piyabha Kongsamut, Kristina Kostial, Victoria Summers, and Athanasios Vamvakidis. 2000.

186. Anticipating Balance of Payments Crises: The Role of Early Warning Systems, by Andrew Berg, Eduardo Borensztein, Gian Maria Milesi-Ferretti, and Catherine Pattillo. 1999.

185. Oman Beyond the Oil Horizon: Policies Toward Sustainable Growth, edited by Ahsan Mansur and Volker Treichel. 1999.

Note: For information on the titles and availability of Occasional Papers not listed, please consult the IMF's *Publications Catalog* or contact IMF Publication Services.

231

ISBN 1-58906-325-

Chile:
Institutions and Policies Underpinning
Stability and Growth

9 781589 063259